D0019196

A Phaidon Theatre Manual

A Phaidon Theatre Manual
STAGE MANAGEMENT AND THEATRE ADMINISTRATION
PAULINE MENEAR
AND TERRY HAWKINS

Series Editor: David Mayer

Acknowledgements
The author and the publisher gratefully acknowledge
the help and assistance of the students and staff at the
Royal Academy of Dramatic Art, London, for their
participation in the photographs taken by Michael Prior.
They would further like to thank the Oxford Stage
Company for allowing Carol Baugh to photograph the
dress rehearsal and the opening night of their
production of *The Miracle Plays*.

Photographs: Carol Baugh pp. 15, 93, 97, 113; Michael
Prior pp. 16-17, 53, 64, 81, 103.

Illustrations: Jones, Sewell and Associates pp. 20, 22,
26, 31, 34, 44-45, 47, 54, 57, 60, 61, 66, 77; Miller,
Craig and Cocking pp. 10, 11-12, 13-14, 21, 24-25, 29,
32-33, 36-37, 68-69, 86-87, 88-89, 95; The Drawing
Room, Warwick p. 105.

Phaidon Press Limited
Regent's Wharf
All Saints Street
London N1 9PA

First published 1988
Revised edition 1993
Reprinted 1995, 1998, 1999

© 1993 Phaidon Press Limited

ISBN 0 7148 2516 6

A CIP catalogue record for this book is available from
the British Library.

All rights reserved. No part of this publication may be
reproduced, stored in a retrieval system or transmitted,
in any form or by any means, electronic, mechanical,
photocopying, recording or otherwise, without the prior
permission of Phaidon Press Limited.

Printed in Singapore

Contents

INTRODUCTION

Work in the theatre is always undertaken with a future performance in mind, but two artistic facts of life affect this work. One is that no one, no matter how naturally talented and accomplished, can invariably count on inspiration to solve a problem. The other fact is that time is the most precious of all theatrical commodities. The date of a first performance is an unalterable deadline, and that deadline, in turn, determines a whole sequence of earlier deadlines which must be met within the resources, not always ideal, that are available to the theatrical team.

These facts have been our starting-point in devising this series. Inspiration may be rare, but creativity, we suggest, can be supplemented by technique. Effective organization coupled with careful forward-planning can result in impressive productions. Experience has shown that good preparation will actually free the creative imagination and give it room to flourish.

This series has been designed to meet the needs of those working in the non-professional theatre, that is students and undergraduates, school teachers, and members of amateur dramatic and operatic societies. This is not an indication of the standards of the performances to be achieved; some amateur productions are quite outstanding. In fact some of the differences between the amateur and the professional are in the amateurs' favour: amateur groups can often call upon enormous resources for behind-the-scenes labour and the large casts that are so often out of reach of most professional companies. But non-professionals are more likely to be limited by the amount of time, money, space and materials available. We recognize that you will be working with some or all of these advantages and restrictions, and we offer ways of looking at problems which will stimulate the imagination and produce solutions. The answers will then be yours, not ours.

Putting on a play is essentially teamwork, teamwork which depends upon the creativity of administrators and craftsmen, performers, directing staff and stage crews. The team can best thrive when responsibilities are shared and lines of communiciation are always open, direct and cordial. In recognition of these needs we have linked the books by planning charts and repeating themes looked at from different angles in order to emphasize that the best results are always achieved when skills are pooled.

Dozens of performances and hours of discussion lie behind these texts, and while we cannot claim to have covered every eventuality, we are confident that the approach outlined in the following pages will lead to productions that are successful, imaginative, and, above all, enjoyable for you, your colleagues, and your audiences.

David Mayer

Safety

Attention to safety is vitally important when you are putting on any production. When there is a procedure in this book where special care must be taken a safety flash has been inserted in the margin.

CHAPTER I

THE ROLE OF STAGE MANAGEMENT

Staging a play or a musical can be exciting, demanding and rewarding. It can also be exhausting, frustrating and chaotic. But a good stage management team can turn a potentially embarrassing production into a smooth-running, trouble-free success.

The stage management team is the channel of communication between all the people and departments contributing to a production. They are the organizers who ensure that everybody and everything is in its right place at the right time. They document every onstage move by anybody or anything during the production. They must be calm in a crisis, patient with frayed tempers, and infinitely understanding of everyone's problems.

As stage manager you must be versatile, and in a small organization that lacks a full technical or design team you may need to undertake all sorts of jobs such as building and painting a set, perhaps lighting it, supplying sound effects, props and furniture and operating the lighting and sound control desks.

Even in a larger organization with full resources it is important for every stage management team member to have a good working knowledge of everyone else's job in order to co-ordinate all the departments successfully by appreciating and anticipating their needs and problems.

Stage managers must also be physically resilient; even the best-organized production will need many hours of hard work to reach a standard that everyone can be proud of. Lastly they need to be adaptable, flexible and mentally alert. In the theatre things rarely go exactly as planned, and there will always be last-minute problems and changes to be coped with.

THE TEAM

A stage management team can number between two and twelve, depending on the people available and the work to be done, but whatever the team's size work must be fairly shared and the members organized so as not to waste their time and energy.

The list of job titles and descriptions below is a framework around which to organize your team. It can be adapted to accommodate any number of people by doubling up jobs and responsibilities as suggested.

PRODUCTION MANAGER (PM)

■ always: the senior member of the technical/ production team; in control of the production budget; responsible for the building and transportation of the set; in charge of technical liaison on tour
■ sometimes: in charge of the fit-up (load-in) of the set on stage and the get-out (load-out)
■ can double as: TSM and SM
■ qualities: experience in all aspects of technical theatre; ability to keep to a budget and negotiate.

TECHNICAL STAGE MANAGER (TSM) (Technical director)

■ always: in charge of the technical aspects of the stage; runs the fit-up and get-out; in charge of the stage staff and stock scenery
■ can double as: carpenter, PM or SM
■ qualities: good knowledge of carpentry and stage mechanics.

COMPANY MANAGER (CM)

■ always: in charge of the welfare of the acting and stage management company; organizes their transport and accommodation on tour and liaises with venue on box office returns and publicity; pays any wages; is eyes and ears of director when not present
■ can double as: stage manager
■ qualities: good at figures, tact, patience.

STAGE MANAGER (SM) (Production SM)

■ always: senior member of the SM team; controls props/furniture budget; sees that all information coming out of rehearsal reaches the right department and the PM; in charge backstage during show; organizes scene changes and stage staff
■ sometimes: runs rehearsals and cues the show; finds props; fits up and paints the set.
■ can double as: any member of the team
■ qualities: good all-round knowledge; experience with actors and directors.

DEPUTY STAGE MANAGER (DSM) (First assistant SM)

■ usually: in charge of the prompt script; running rehearsals; cueing the show and dealing with paper work involved
■ sometimes: in charge of running backstage if SM is 'on-the-book'; in charge of props if ASM is inexperienced
■ can double as: SM and ASM.
■ qualities: some knowledge of all technical departments; must enjoy working with actors and directors.

ASSISTANT STAGE MANAGER (ASM) (Second assistant SM)

■ always: most involved with propping; in charge of setting and running the props in performance; assists DSM in rehearsal
■ sometimes: involved in scene changes; helps to fit up, paint and dress the set
■ qualities: boundless energy.

PROP DEPARTMENT

This is not strictly part of the stage management team as its responsibilities are limited to those set out below.

■ always: makes props, dressing and furniture as necessary, often to designer's brief.
■ sometimes: in charge of all prop acquisition; prop budget; storage and cataloguing of stock props and furniture

Pre-production Period

Function	Pre-rehearsal Period
Administrator	Check play available for performance. Check score available for performance. Check venue available. Negotiate royalty payments. Pre-production discussions with Director and Designers. Check licensing and permission, especially firearms. Check credit card registration. Gather programme material. Plan publicity. Announce auditions. Determine budget.
Director	Pre-production discussions. Conduct auditions – with choreographer and Musical Director. Announce casting. Announce and initiate rehearsal schedules.
Production Manager/ Technical Director	Pre-production budget meeting with Administration. Design meeting with Director, Designer and Stage Manager. Appoint Stage Manager and technical staff.
Stage Management	Attend design meeting and run auditions. Find a rehearsal space. Prepare prompt copy and provisional lists. Research with designer. Gather rehearsal props, furniture and set.
Scenic Design and Construction	Pre-production discussions. Model making: technical and working. Prepare drawings. Prepare prop drawings. Get Director's approval. Prepare castings and planning.
Lighting	Pre-production discussions. Read and re-read text. Research & Planning costume and scene.
Sound	Pre-production discussions. Read and re-read text. Prepare a selection of provisional tapes. Get Director's approval.
Music	Check availability of scores. Agree rehearsal schedule with Director. Organize a rehearsal pianist. Audition singers. Gather orchestra.
Choreography Fights	Check rehearsal space. Agree rehearsal schedule with Director. Organize rehearsal pianist. Audition dancers.
Costume Design and Construction	Pre-production discussions. Costume research and drawing. Working drawings for wigs/hats/shoes. Fabric sampling. Costing and planning.

Function	Week 6	Week 5	Week 4	Week 3
Administration	Gather programme material. Display publicity material. Open booking if necessary.	Start press stories. Monitor publicity. Monitor bookings. Contact with rehearsals.	Recruit FOH staff if required. Invite critics.	Direct sell.
Director	Attend production meeting. ■ Discussions ■ Script cuts ■ Note running time.	Blocking rehearsal.	Business rehearsals. Rehearsal props introduced. Attend meetings. Listen to sound tape. Lighting meeting	Singers and dancers integrated. Reblocking. ■ Pianist present. Orchestral rehearsal
Production Manager	Costing meetings with set, prop and costume makers. Production meeting. Problem solving and budget decisions.	Coordinating technical departments and budget control.		Progress meeting. Arrange for equipment hir Liaison with venue.
Stage Management	Mark out and prepare rehearsal space. Note script changes. Attend production and props meetings.	Run rehearsal Prop, furniture and dressings search and making. Liaison with all departments.		Attend progress meeting. Arrange sound and lighting meetings for director
Scenic design and construction	Meetings and planning with technical director. ■ Attend read through Call for actors, staff and workshop. Scenic construction and propmaking.	Liaison with SM and workshop. ■ Buy soft furnishings.	■ Choose hire furniture and scene painting.	Drawings for new props. Alterations as necessary.
Costume design and construction make up	Attend first rehearsal.	Check stock Measure all actors Buy fabrics Order wigs	Preliminary fittings Cutting and making	Keep in touch with rehearsals for new costume ideas Sort shoes
Lighting	Attend production meeting. Keep in contact rehearsals – SM/Director/Designer. Liaison with Director and Designer	Artwork and photography for projection. ■ Construction special lighting affects.	■ Check stock.	Attend rehearsal and run through.
Sound	Attend production meeting. Basic provisional tape in rehearsal.	Research and planning. ■ Check stock and buy in tapes, effects records, etc. Meeting with director.	Prepare effects tapes. Sound meetings with director.	Record special effects. Record hire effects with actors. ■ Design sound rig. ■ Hire equipment.
Music	Singing rehearsals. Music rehearsals.			Singers join main rehearsals
Choreography and fights	Dancing rehearsals. Fight rehearsals.		Hire weapons with SM.	Fights choreographed. Dancers join main rehearsa

Week 2	Day 7	Day 6	Day 5	Day 4	Day 3	Day 2	Day 1
Invite press to photocall.	Check Box. Engage FOH staff. ■ Ushers. ■ Sales. ■ Box Office.	Train FOH staff. Arrange FOH displays. Print programmes.				Photo call.	
Polish rehearsal. ■ Fights in rehearsal. Meet to discuss lighting. Meet with sound dept, to check final FX.	Introduce performance props.		Run through	Attend lighting and sound plotting sessions.	Attend technical rehearsal and give notes.	Photo call, dress rehearsal give notes.	Final dress rehearsal and gives notes.
Make up production schedule. Arrange transport and staff for the get in/fit up and show staff.	Supervise get in and fit up as per production schedule	Continue fit up as per schedule (+ LX main rig).	Continue as per schedule. Possible fire inspection	Supervise schedule. (LX and sound plotting sessions).	Attend technical rehearsal.	Supervise technical work on stage. Attend dress rehearsal.	Supervise technical work on stage. Attend final dress rehearsal.
Arrange lighting designer to see an early run through. Director to listen to sound tape. Prepare setting lists and cue sheets.	Run rehearsals. Team attend run through. Finalize setting lists, cue sheets	Help fit up paint etc. Final props adjustments.	Team help move out of rehearsal rooms to venue.	Dress the set Set the props. Attend LX and sound plotting sessions.	Possible scene change rehearsal. Run technical rehearsal.	Run Dress rehearsal. Attend Director's note session.	Run final dress rehearsal.
Prop meetings to check all props. Attend Lighting Discussion.	Fit up and painting as per production.	Continue fit up and painting as per production schedule.	Fit up and paint end texture as per schedule.	Attend lighting session and LX plotting. Dress the set.	Attend technical rehearsal.	Attend photo call. Attend dress rehearsal.	Technical work as necessary. Attend dress rehearsal.
Accessories found/bought Second or final fittings	Check costumes, Check wigs arrived.	Get in for costumes. Costumes to dressing rooms.	Attend run through.	Attend run through. Check make up.	Attend technical rehearsal. Check make up under lights.		
	Finalize copy lighting design. Preliminary rigging. Hired equipment arrives.	Lighting rigging.	Focusing of lighting.	Lighting session plotting.	Technical rehearsal.	Dress rehearsal. Attend notes sessions. Technical work on stage.	Final dress rehearsal. Technical work on stage.
Preparation of final tapes. ■ Rehearse live sound mixing – mini-tech. Director to hear tape.	Hired equipment arrives. Mini sound tech with orchestra.	Sound rigging.	Attend run through.	Sound plotting rework tapes.	Technical rehearsal. Rework tapes.	Dress rehearsal. Rework tapes. Attend notes session.	Final dress rehearsal. Attend notes session.
Musicians rehearse with sound reinforcement if necessary.				Rehearsal for orchestra and cast.	Technical rehearsal, piano only.	Dress rehearsal with orchestra.	
Fights join main rehearsal.		Choreographer present as needed.					

The Run and Post Production

Function	The Run	Post Production
Administrator	Show reports to Director. FOH staff checks. Monitor sales. Liaise with Stage Manager.	File prompt script and production paperwork. Collect scripts. Pay accounts.
Director	Note running times. Director's notes to cast. Warnings and encouragement before performance. Keep contact with SM for problems.	File director's script. Compile report on production and contact list for cast or production team.
Production Manager	Work on budget accounts with Administration.	Arrange transport and staff for get-out. Supervise get-out and storage of any stock set. Supervise returns of hired/borrowed equipment. Final work on accounts with Administration
Stage Management	Run shows as per prompt script, running lists, etc. Check set, props, furniture settings. Supervise understudy rehearsals. Show reports.	Get out props, dressings and furniture. Supervise return of hired and borrowed items and stock to stores. Assemble prompt script and all lists, plots, etc. for the show and file with Administration.
Scenic Design and Construction		Sort out scenic stock to keep with Production Manager.
Lighting	Check performances crew present. Check equipment pre-performance. Run Show.	Dismantle and store lighting equipment. Return hired equipment. File lighting plot.
Sound	Check performances crew present. Check equipment pre-performance. Run Show.	Dismantle and store sound equipment. Store tapes and catalogue for future. Return hired equipment.
Costume Design		Cleaning and storage of costumes. File costume Bible.

THE TEAM

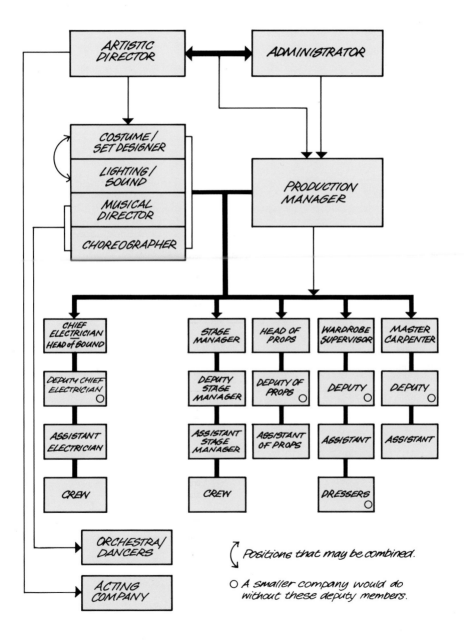

ARTISTIC DIRECTOR ↔ ADMINISTRATOR

ARTISTIC DIRECTOR →
- COSTUME / SET DESIGNER
- LIGHTING / SOUND
- MUSICAL DIRECTOR
- CHOREOGRAPHER

ADMINISTRATOR → PRODUCTION MANAGER

PRODUCTION MANAGER:
- CHIEF ELECTRICIAN HEAD of SOUND
  - DEPUTY CHIEF ELECTRICIAN ○
  - ASSISTANT ELECTRICIAN
  - CREW
- STAGE MANAGER
  - DEPUTY STAGE MANAGER
  - ASSISTANT STAGE MANAGER
  - CREW
- HEAD OF PROPS
  - DEPUTY OF PROPS ○
  - ASSISTANT OF PROPS
- WARDROBE SUPERVISOR
  - DEPUTY ○
  - ASSISTANT
  - DRESSERS ○
- MASTER CARPENTER
  - DEPUTY ○
  - ASSISTANT

ORCHESTRA / DANCERS

ACTING COMPANY

⌇ Positions that may be combined.

○ A smaller company would do without these deputy members.

CHAPTER 2

BEFORE REHEARSALS

Stage management should try to stay one step ahead of the needs of the director and acting company by planning, preparing and organizing in advance. You should start as soon as possible, ideally even before rehearsals begin. (In some organizations this may not be possible, in which case you should try to cover the relevant areas in this section as soon as you can.)

PUTTING THE TEAM TOGETHER

Before volunteering yourself or electing someone for any job on the team, give some thought to the kind of qualities and experience required to do that job well. The PM and SM (PSM) should be elected first so that they can be instrumental in the choice of the rest of their team and so that they can be available to do the advance planning.

Try to create a balanced team again bearing in mind the experience, abilities and talents of each individual. A stage manager who is comfortable working on stage and dealing with technical problems should be paired with a deputy stage manager who enjoys working with people. An assistant stage manager who has a talent for making props should be paired with someone who is good at persuading people to lend or give them.

No matter what the size of the team it is most important that every member works together. They should be considerate of one another and always prepared to lend a hand when it is needed. In the end it does not matter who has done what, provided the team has got the job done and done well.

Above all they should be people who will enjoy working together and who will put the production before any differences of opinion or clashes of personality.

PLANNING

By the time the stage management team is required the dates of performances and theatre/venue will have been decided upon, and the director and designer will have been working together for quite some time to decide on the style the production will take. The designer will have put her ideas together in the form of a set model and costume and props sketches.

The production manager will have been allocated a production budget by the administrator, and no further progress can be made until the production manager calls a design meeting with the director, designer and stage manager if available. The director and designer can then present their design ideas to the production manager who must decide whether they are feasible in terms of the production budget and the time and personnel available.

In order to do this the production manager should consult with the carpentry, wardrobe and props experts who will be working on the production. They must estimate how much money and time it will take to produce their part of the design and report back to the production manager. Should it turn out that the design is too expensive and should it not be possible to increase the production budget the director and designer may have to rethink their ideas. It is therefore essential that the design meeting be held as soon as possible before rehearsals begin.

Assuming that all is well the designer will go ahead and prepare the working drawings and ground plan, and the production manager will discuss the schedule with the director. The production or stage schedule will only be provisional at this stage as much consultation with all technical departments has to to take place before it can be finalized. The production manager and director should decide how much stage time to allow for the technical and dress rehearsal and whether any extra time on stage might be available. The director can then go ahead and work out a rehearsal schedule.

The stage manager will need the answers to some vital questions before rehearsals begin.

■ does the director have any special requirements beyond the usual needs of a rehearsal? (For example, source material for the acting company such as literature, video tapes or films and visits to theatre/cinema.)

■ does the director have any special requirements in the way of rehearsal space? Will she need the space marked out, and rehearsal props and furniture available on the first day?

■ does the director have a rehearsal schedule and are there any cuts or changes in the script?

■ are there any extra props, furniture or effects other than those mentioned in the script and does the period and style of your production differ from that in which the play was written?

The SM (PSM) should then study the set design and obtain copies of the ground plan and scale working drawings for props.

The stage management team should research into the period and style of the production with the aid of books, art galleries, museums, exhibitions etc., so that they are able to work along the same lines as the director and designer.

AUDITIONS

The director will need to hold readings or auditions to cast the play. The administrator will advertise for actors if necessary or contact society or club members. Stage management may be called upon to organize and run these events.

Preparation

Choose a room that is clean, reasonably comfortable and away from too much noise or disturbance. If possible arrange for a second room close by in which the auditionees can wait until they are called. Make sure toilet facilities are available.

Contact auditionees with the time and place of their auditions and details of any special pieces or songs that the director requires them to perform.

Provide a table and chairs for the auditioners and a spare table and chairs for use in the auditionees' performances if required. If a piano is needed make sure it is in tune.

In the case of a reading make sure there are plenty of copies of the script.

Running

Ensure you have a list of names and audition times.

Check that you have the auditionees' correct addresses and telephone numbers before they leave.

The director may want auditionees to read a particular piece – make sure you have plenty of clean, legible copies.

Some auditionees may want you to prompt or read in other parts for them. If so get a copy of their script from them and familiarize yourself with it.

Wait until the previous auditionee has left the audition room before entering. If the auditioners are ready show the next candidate in, announcing their name as they enter. Leave the room unless you are needed to prompt or read in.

It may fall to you to be the one to tell auditionees whether or not they are to be recalled for a second audition. Always be tactful and sensitive, but businesslike and reasonably detached. Generally speaking do not get too involved with any one auditionee or you may be giving them an advantage over the others.

COMPANY LIAISON

Compile a list of addresses and telephone numbers of *everyone* connected with the production, including venues (theatre, office, rehearsal rooms and so on).

Once the play has been cast and the actors offered their parts it is your task to liaise with them to ensure they are always in the right place at the right time. See that:

■ all actors and departments have a copy of the script and/or score, the rehearsal schedule and list of contact addresses and phone numbers

■ all actors are informed of any reading or research the director wants them to do

■ everyone knows the time and place of the first rehearsal. Draw a simple map of the area with the rehearsal room marked on it with details of bus routes and stations and send a copy to everyone.

PREPARING FOR REHEARSAL

This involves working on the script, supplying any props or furniture the actors need to work with, finding and preparing the rehearsal room.

Never take any performance props, furniture, costumes or pieces of set for rehearsal without getting permission from the relevant department. Be ready to return them on request if work still needs doing to them.

THE SCRIPT

Every member of the team should *read the play* before rehearsals begin. The SM, or whoever is to take charge of rehearsals, should make up the *prompt script* with all its accompanying lists and charts. The team also needs to work through the script noting down all the props, furniture, dressing, sound and special effects mentioned. These are usually found in the stage directions but close attention should also be paid to the dialogue as not all plays contain comprehensive directions. Any extra props or effects that the director and designer want should be added to the lists. These are only *provisional lists*; many of the items on them may be changed or cut as rehearsals progress. But they are essential at this stage if you are to supply props and furniture for rehearsals.

PROPS AND FURNITURE

Ideally the acting company should rehearse with the articles they will be using on stage. This is not always possible – they may not have been obtained at this stage, and valuable and/or breakable articles should not be used until the last moment. But it is essential to provide some kind of substitute for *everything*, as close in size and weight to the real thing as possible.

Pieces of wood cut to size and labelled, or plastic and paper replicas are all acceptable. Liquid in bottles, tea pots or glasses should be provided – water will do, but make sure it is fresh every day and that all drinking vessels are clean. Bread, fruit or soup can be used as an inexpensive substitute food – again make sure it is fresh and kept hygienically.

The furniture found in the rehearsal room can be adapted for use: three chairs tied together to form a sofa, or stools tied together to form a bed. But check the size of the actual furniture as soon as possible – tables vary in size and shape, and the sofa and chairs may need to have arms. If cupboards, shelves, chimneypieces or window sills on the set are to be used to put props on, make sure you provide some kind of substitute surface for rehearsal.

SETS AND COSTUMES

Freestanding door boxes, window boxes and chimneypieces held up by a stage brace and weight can often be very useful. Rostra (platforms) and treads may also be used to represent raised areas. Rehearsal costumes: hats, cloaks, belts and swords, coats or long skirts may be available from the wardrobe department.

PROVISIONAL FURNITURE LIST		
SHOW THE THREEPENNY OPERA		SHEET NO. 1
DIRECTOR		
DESIGNER		
STAGE MANAGER		
ITEM	SCENE/PAGE	INFORMATION
LECTERN	SC. 1	Pulpit/desk
HIGH STOOL	SC. 1	
HARPSICHORD	SC. 2	Rosewood. Legs to be sawn off every performance
RENAISSANCE SOFA	SC. 2	
1 CHAIR	SC. 2	Louis XIV
1 CHAIR	SC. 2	Chippendale
GRANDFATHER CLOCK	SC. 2	Chippendale
PLANKS AND 2 OIL DRUMS		to make into a table
BED	SC. 4	Single, plus bedding
TABLE		
CHAIR		
SOFA	SC. 5	
TABLE		
6 CHAIRS		

Provisional Prop List

THE THREEPENNY OPERA

SHOW

DIRECTOR

DESIGNER

STAGE MANAGER

PROP	PAGE/SCENE	INFORMATION
	Scene 1	
SWORDSTICK	4	Macheath (personal)
		('Give and it shall be given unto you.')
LARGE SIGN	6	
BIBLE	6	Peachum
MAP OF THE CITY OF LONDON	7	
BUSINESS CARDS	7	Peachum (personal)
5 WAX DUMMIES	8	1 with arm stump, 1 with medals, 1 with dark glasses.
SEVERAL COINS		
PAPER MONEY		
CANDLE WAX		
IRON		
IRONING BOARD		
REVOLVER		
LANTERN		
2 KNIVES and 14 FORKS		

Provisional Sound Cue List

Show   THE THREEPENNY OPERA

Director

Stage Manager

EFFECT	LENGTH	SCENE/PAGE	
1. Large van driving up and stopping			
2. Alarm bell	?	2	12
3. Drum roll - heralding an execution (possibly live)	30 seconds?	6	39
4. Same	5 seconds	8	57
	?		61
	?		63
			59
			59
			79

PROVISIONAL LIVE EFFECTS

SHOW

THE THREEPENNY OPERA

DIRECTOR

STAGE MANAGER

EFFECT	LENGTH	SCENE/PAGE
Smoke (Smoke gun LX)		
Drum roll - heralding execution		Preset at end of ACT 1.
Same (possibly recorded)	5 secs	
Same	?	P 57
	?	P 61
Loud doorknock offstage (USL)		P 63
Flash and puff of smoke (USR)		P 60
		Sc 9 Page 80

THE REHEARSAL ROOM

If you cannot rehearse on stage you will need to find a suitable room or space. There are many things to consider – ask yourself the following questions:

■ how large? – the room should be as large as your stage/set/acting area with space to spare
■ how many? – musicals may need extra rooms for music and choreography
■ how long for? – note that the director may want to rehearse after the opening night and the stage may not be available
■ when? – if the room is not available for every rehearsal you may need to find others
■ how much? – can you afford this?
■ how accessible? – is it near public transport and are there adequate parking facilities?
■ is it possible to erect some of the set in it? If so are the doors large enough to get it in?
■ can you leave props or furniture in place or will they have to be cleared away?
■ are the acoustics suitable for music?
■ is there a piano? Is it in tune and in good condition?
■ is the floor suitable for dancing? Are there any pillars or other obstructions?

■ are there toilet and changing facilities? If you need to hold costume fittings is there a mirror and somewhere to hang costumes?
■ is there a room nearby where actors can relax and make tea and coffee? Or are there refreshments facilities in the building?
■ are there restaurants, cafés or shops close by?
■ is the light, heat and ventilation adequate?
■ are there enough electric sockets?
■ can the room be blacked out? – you may need to show slides
■ is the room reasonably soundproof? – you may be disturbed by noise from adjoining rooms or busy roads. Does anyone mind how much noise you make?
■ is there a telephone you can use? Will it take incoming and outgoing calls? What is the number?
■ can you use tape to mark out, or will it damage the floor?
■ how much furniture is there in the room? Will you have to bring any more?
■ how do you gain access? Can you have a key? if not when will the building/room be open and when does it close?
■ who cleans the room? Is basic cleaning equipment available?

REHEARSAL KIT

In order to stay one jump ahead of the needs of your director and acting company you need to arm yourself with a number of useful items:

Essentials
- prompt script
- extra paper, pencils, pens
- spare scripts, rehearsal schedule
- notebook, pencil sharpener, erasers
- kettle/cups/coffee/tea/sugar/milk/spoons
- coins for telephone, parking meter
- stop-watch or watch with second hand
- mark-out kit and ground plan
- ashtrays and wastepaper bin
- contact list and map of local area
- extension cord and adapters
- matches
- set model (first day)
- screwdriver and pliers
- adhesive tape and scissors
- tables for director/DSM, props, coffee
- rehearsal furniture
- enough chairs to seat company and any visitors

Possible extras
- spare toilet paper, towel, soap
- first aid kit
- sewing repair kit
- corkscrew/bottle opener
- liquid soap and cloths
- dictionary and diary
- tape/cassette recorder
- flashlight
- telephone/bell ring device
- movie projector/slide projector
- video recorder
- blackout material/curtains
- mirror and costume rail (for fittings)
- lockable storage boxes for props
- cleaning equipment (brooms, etc.).

Try to make the rehearsal space as much like the performance space as possible. Use as much of the real set as you can and whatever furniture and props are available.

PREPARING THE REHEARSAL ROOM

Using the ground plan of the set supplied by the designer mark out the dimensions of the acting area on the floor of the room.

Place any door or window boxes and rostra (platforms) you want to use according to their position on the plan. On an open stage or set place objects such as two tables or two chairs to mark the position of the proscenium arch walls.

Put tables either side of the mark-up on which to lay out props.

Set out tables and chairs facing the set for the director and DSM, with the latter nearest the telephone and door if possible.

Lay out refreshments on a separate table near an electric socket if possible and out of the way of the acting space (if there is no extra room or kitchen available).

Set out extra chairs for the use of the acting company, preferably near the doors and coffee-making facilities so that they do not need to walk across the acting area.

Should the rehearsal room be new to your company put up a series of signs and arrows guiding them to it from the street. Do the same for toilet facilities.

Establish a notice board on the wall behind the DSM and near the door and display:

☑ *GROUNDPLAN*

☑ *REHEARSAL SCHEDULE*

☑ *REHEARSAL CALLS*

☑ *CHARACTER/SCENE BREAKDOWN CHART*

☑ *MAPS*

☑ *ANY OTHER RELEVANT INFORMATION*

MARKING OUT

The director and acting company need to have the acting space accurately defined for them and features of the set clearly positioned. The designer's ground plan is a scaled-down drawing of the position the set will take on the floor of the stage. With the aid of a scale rule you can scale up these drawings to their actual size and transfer them to the rehearsal-room floor in the form of tape or chalk lines.

Three people are best to do a mark out (lay out) – one to read the plan with the aid of a scale rule (this is the most difficult job) and two to mark out (one holding the end of the tape measure and one reading the measurement and marking the floor).

First measure the dimensions of the room. Then measure the dimensions of the set from the plan. Will the set fit into the room and is there room to spare?

Position the mark up in the room leaving plenty of extra space all around it, particularly at the front – the director will not want to be too close to the actors.

Take into account any pillars or other obstructions in the room. If they cannot be avoided you may be able to incorporate them into the set – say as the proscenium arch walls.

Should the set be too big for the room consult your director before marking out. He may not need the whole set as it appears on the ground plan – the main acting area may be enough. If the whole set is required it may be possible to superimpose the outer parts on top of the main acting area by marking them in a different colour.

Likewise, if the play has more than one set – say a different one for each act, you can mark each one out on top of one another using a different colour. (Make sure to display a colour/act key along with the ground plan.)

If possible use brightly coloured tape so that the marking will show up well. Should you not be allowed to use tape on the floor mark out with chalk lines instead. But put a small piece of tape in every corner so that you can re-mark the line without having to measure again when the chalk wears off. Should the room be carpeted and/or the markings have to be taken up after every rehearsal, use pre-measured strips of string or cloth tape pinned or held down with small pieces of adhesive tape.

If the furniture positions are marked on the plan transfer these to the floor of the room as well. (These positions may change and need to be re-marked as rehearsals progress.)

READING YOUR SCALE RULE

The ground plan is drawn to scale – this should be clearly marked on the plan. The most common scales are shown below. The metric ruler is a specific 1:25 scale rule similar to the one on the opposite page – to scale up your plan no calculations are required. Alternatively, an ordinary metric ruler can be used, in which case, each unit must be multiplied by 25. To scale up a 1:24 plan use either an imperial ruler and multiply each unit by 24, as shown in the diagram, or a 1:24 scale rule.

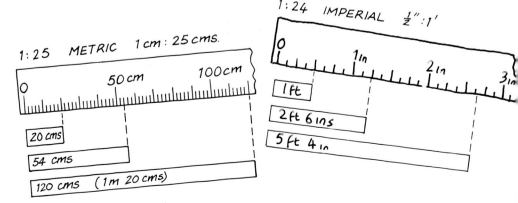

MARKING OUT EQUIPMENT

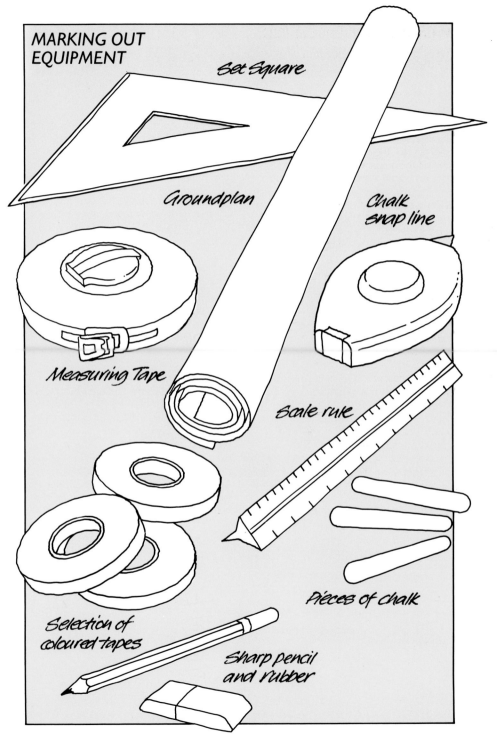

Set Square

Groundplan

Chalk snap line

Measuring Tape

Scale rule

Pieces of chalk

Selection of coloured tapes

Sharp pencil and rubber

MARKING OUT METHODS

There are two basic methods of marking out. For greatest accuracy use one method to do the initial mark out and the other to check your measurements.

USING TWO FIXED POINTS

This method is most useful when marking out your set on the stage. It ensures that the set is put in the correct position in relation to the fixed points of the building.

The most common points to use are the upstage corners of the proscenium arch walls. To use this method in the rehearsal room first mark the 'pros walls' on your floor and take further measurements from them.

Measure from point A to point C on your plan.

Fix or hold the end of the tape at point A on the floor and measure out the appropriate length. Hold a piece of chalk at that point on the tape and scribe an arc.

Repeat the process between point C and D. Where the arcs cross you have the position for point C.

Repeat as necessary for the rest of the set. You may find it easier to tie the chalk on the end of a piece of string and measure that to appropriate lengths instead.

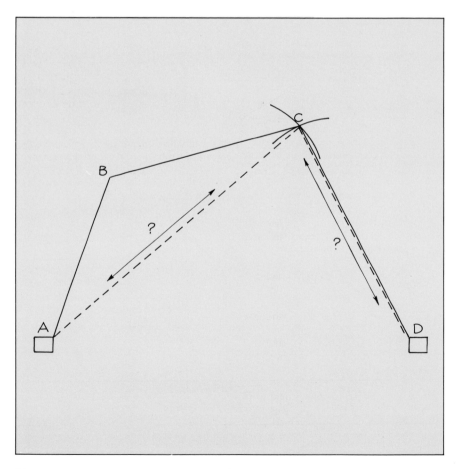

USING SETTING AND CENTRE LINES

The setting line (S/L) is the farthest down-stage line of the acting area on any particular set. The front curtains or tabs drop to this line.

The centre line (C/L) is the line running up and down stage at right angles to S/L and cutting the stage into two equal parts. If these lines are not marked on the plan draw them in yourself.

Measure the S/L and C/L on your plan.

Mark them on the floor of the room using a chalk line or tape. If you have two measuring tapes lay one of them down to form the C/L. Fix it down securely with tape to stop it shifting.

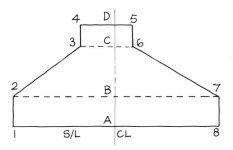

With the aid of a set square draw lines out from the C/L left and right to intersect with the corners of the set.

Measure the distances between A and B, A and C, and A and D.

Mark these positions on the floor with chalk.

Measure the distances between point B and point 2, point B and point 7, point C and point 3 and so on.

Take your second tape measure and place the end at point B. Measure out stage right (SR) the prescribed distance and mark point 2 with chalk. Repeat until you have all corners marked.

To doublecheck your measurements follow the same process using the setting line instead of the centre line.

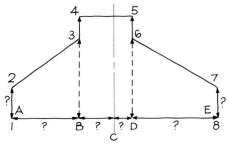

Join all the marks with tape to form the walls of your set.

To determine the positions of doors and windows, snap a chalk line and measure along that.

Mark the solid parts of the wall with tape. Leave a gap for the door and a line of tape to show which way the door opens. Leave a dotted line for the window opening. If door and window boxes are marked on the plan mark these in too.

Mark furniture by placing two short pieces of tape at right angles at each upstage corner of every piece (see plan on next page).

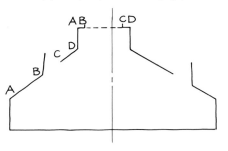

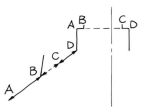

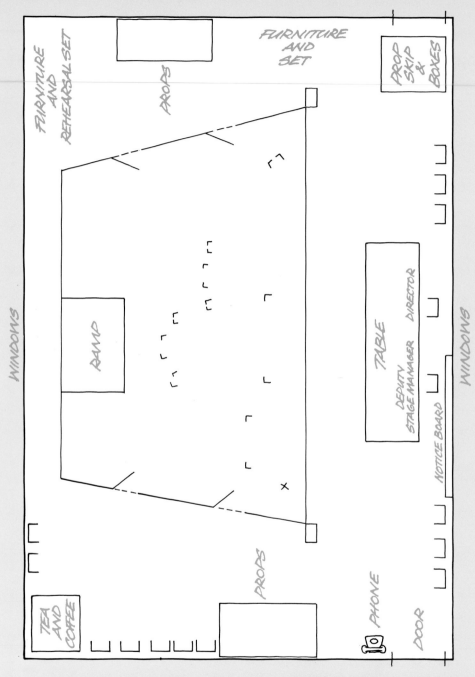

REHEARSAL ROOM MARKED OUT FOR THE THREEPENNY OPERA. ACT 2. SC5.

CHAPTER 3

DURING REHEARSALS

INSIDE THE REHEARSAL ROOM

The rehearsal room must always be ready by the time the first member of the company arrives. The stage management team should arrive at least half an hour before the acting company's call; and well before that if there is still work to be done, which is likely to be the case on the first day.

FIRST DAY

Lay out chairs for everyone in a semi-circle facing the table on which the set model should be placed. Introduce yourselves to everyone as they arrive making sure you have their correct address and telephone number.

The first day is unique and usually takes the following form:

■ talk by the director and designer to describe the production, set and costume designs to the company. They will need the set model and possibly costume and prop sketches. Make sure they all arrive safely. This may be the last time they will be available for use in rehearsal as they will be needed by the various technical departments thereafter. Should your director wish to use them again make arrangements with the departments to borrow them and make sure they are returned promptly

■ read-through of the play. Time the read-through and be prepared to read in parts for any missing actors. The director will also

inform the company of any cuts or alterations made to the script. Whoever is in charge of the prompt script (usually the DSM) must take note of these changes. The prompt script must be accurate

■ the director may have also broken the play down into working units. Most plays are already divided into acts and scenes, but not all. The director may also wish to subdivide existing acts into smaller units and will number or name each unit according to its content.

DAILY ROUTINE

The stage management team should meet together before the rehearsal begins, in plenty of time to prepare the room and discuss any problems that may have arisen from the previous rehearsal.

First check that all relevant doors are unlocked, and heating, ventilation and lighting provided. Then:

■ make sure that the room is clean and ashtrays laid out (if smoking is allowed and the director has no objection)

■ wash any dirty cups; put the kettle on

■ lay out the furniture and props for the first scene to be rehearsed that day

■ offer everyone tea or coffee as they arrive

■ let the director know as soon as everyone has arrived so that work can start. Should anyone be missing try to contact them at home. Start without them if they are going to be much delayed

■ at the end of rehearsal the team should

meet again to discuss any problems. This is often the best time to ask the director questions

■ if the room is to be used by another group before your next rehearsal make sure you leave it clean and tidy. Stack all your furniture out of the way and pack props and costumes into lockable storage skips (boxes). Take up string or cloth tape mark outs.

RUNNING THE REHEARSAL ROOM

Furniture and scenery

Mark the position of scene changes in the prompt script.

Make up furniture setting lists/diagrams for every act/scene.

Mark all furniture positions on to the rehearsal room floor.

Set up the furniture and any props for each scene as it is to be rehearsed. (If your setting list is accurate and clear the ASM will be able to help.)

Keep your SM informed of any changes or additions to furniture or set.

Pay close attention to how the director is using the furniture and set. For example if a sofa is to be tipped over backwards, the one being borrowed or hired must be suitable.

Props

Make up prop setting lists for each act/scene.

Lay out props on prop tables as they would be in the theatre.

Set up the props for each act/scene as it is to be rehearsed.

Inform your SM of any changes or additions, again paying close attention to how the prop is being used: this may affect the way it has to be made.

If at all possible use the actual props in rehearsal as soon as they are ready.

Effects

Mark the positions of any sound or special effects in the prompt script.

Make the sound of door bells or telephones as they come up in rehearsal.

If the director wants to rehearse with recorded sound you will need a tape recorder. Ask whoever is making up the sound tape for the production to make up a tape for rehearsal. You must of course give them a list of what you want.

Inform your SM of any live effects required and make up a list of cues, and of any lighting or special effects required and note provisional cues on the prompt script.

Wardrobe

Make a note of any quick changes and inform your SM.

Pay attention to the way costumes are being used. Pockets of a size to accommodate a particular prop may need to be added to a garment, or blood may be required in a scene which may stain the actors' costumes.

THE REHEARSAL NOTE

A great deal of information needs to find its way out of rehearsal to the appropriate departments. Furthermore, one change or addition may actually affect more than one department (for example a note to the ASM or prop department asking for blood for a particular actor needs a separate note warning the wardrobe department).

To ensure that everyone receives all the information they need, write it down in the form of a rehearsal note. Do this after every rehearsal. Give a copy to your stage manager and keep one for yourself. The SM can then circulate it to all departments. It saves time and energy if you make up several copies of a blank rehearsal note before rehearsals begin so all you have to do is fill them in.

<u>REHEARSAL NOTE</u>

SHOW   THE THREEPENNY OPERA   DIRECTOR   *A.L.W.*

DATE   *10th May*   SM   *D.H.*

SHEET NO   15   DSM   *R.C.*

<u>DESIGN</u>   *Would it be possible for the D/S left door to be hinged to open both ways (swing)?*

<u>PROPS</u>   *ACT I Sc.3. all desk dressing and stool <u>CUT</u>*

              Swagger stick for TIGER BROWN

              Prologue Props – A RUBBER TRUNCHEON
              1 LARGE GREEN UMBRELLA (Peachum)
              1 MEDIUM RED UMBRELLA (Mrs Peachum)
              1 SMALL PINK UMBRELLA (Polly)

<u>WARDROBE</u>   *The 5 dummies will need beggars' costumes – all male. Could Jenny's feather boa be red and very long (2 joined together)?*

<u>LX</u>   *The Director would like a follow spot if possible – and 2 Smoke Guns.*

<u>SOUND</u>   *The drum rolls will be done by the timpanist in the orchestra pit.*

<u>GENERAL</u>   *ACT I is running 1 hour 4 minutes.*
              ACT II – 46 minutes.
              There will be a run of ACT III on Tuesday 15th at 7.p.m.

CALLS

Rehearsal calls

The director will tell you which scenes are to be worked on at the next rehearsal. You may be left to work out for yourself exactly who needs to be called and when.

If you have made up a character/scene breakdown chart your task will be much easier. Keep a version of this with your prompt script. Make a large version for the wall of the rehearsal room. This is vital for plays with large casts where actors are playing more than one part.

Make sure you keep a note of the availability of each member of your cast. Keep the director informed. The director will not want to rehearse a scene if the actor playing the major role is going to be missing. Make sure everybody knows their next call before leaving for the day, or telephone them with their call as soon as you know it.

Write out the next call as in the example below. Display a copy on your group's notice or call board, and one on the wall of the rehearsal room. Keep a copy for yourself and the director.

During rehearsals make sure you know where actors are going before they leave the room so that you can find them quickly when they are needed.

Sometimes directors overrun and are still rehearsing a scene after the time appointed to start the next. Some like to be kept informed of the time in order to stay on schedule; others don't. If in doubt discuss it. Explain the delay to waiting actors. They may want to wait in another room – offer to call them when the director is ready.

Wardrobe calls

Wardrobe calls will be needed if actors are wearing costumes or wigs. Fittings need to be slotted into the rehearsal schedule. Liaise with the wardrobe department with the aid of your stage manager and call actors as they would be for rehearsal.

If possible hold the fittings near the rehearsal room. If not make sure actors know where they have to go and give them a map if necessary.

REHEARSAL CALL

THE THREEPENNY OPERA

SHOW

DATE

PLACE

		MISS TUCKER MRS EVANS
10.30 AM	ACT 2 SC. 5	
	ACT 2 SC. 4	MISS GARDEN MR EVANS
12.00		
	LUNCH BREAK	
1.00 PM	ACT 1 SC 2	MISS GARDEN MR CERQUIRA MR DUFF
2.00 PM		MR EVANS MR HAREWOOD
		MR MCKINVEW TO JOIN
	ACT 1 SC	MISS TUCKER
3.00 PM	SOLOMON SONGS	MISS GARDEN
4.00 PM	ACT 3 SC 8	MISS MCDONNELL
4.30 PM		
	BREAK	FULL COMPANY
5.30 PM	RUN OF ACT 2	

THE PROMPT SCRIPT

The prompt script or book is the production's 'bible'. It should contain enough accurate clear information to enable another stage management team to run an identical production – both in rehearsal and performance. It consists of:

■ an accurate version of the script, including all cuts, rewrites, acting pauses
■ clear and concise 'blocking'
■ all cues – lighting, sound, flys, effects, scene changes – and the details of what each cue does
■ calls for actors and technical stage staff during performance
■ all setting lists, cue sheets, running plots, cast list and charts.

How to make up a prompt script

Obtain two copies of a printed script if possible.

Separate the script into single pages and stick each page on to one side of plain paper punched for filing, leaving as wide a gap as possible on the hole side. The size of the paper depends on the size of the script – A4 is standard.

Protect the holes against tearing with self-adhesive reinforcements.

Put coloured card dividers between each act/scene or affix a tag to the edge of the first page of each scene and label them.

Put into a hard-back ring binder.

If the script is typed (text on one side only) there is no need to put in extra paper.

If only one copy of the printed script is available, photocopy the reverse sides of pages, and make up as described above. Alternatively use the method shown in the example below.

Whatever method you use there should always be a blank page opposite every page of text and, if the size of the script allows, a blank column between the text and the empty page. Insert an extra blank page at the beginning of the script and at the start of the second half (after the intermission) to accommodate pre-show checks.

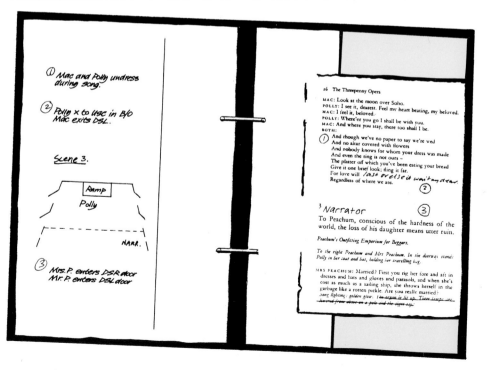

BASIC BLOCKING TECHNIQUES

Taking down the blocking is the recording of the moves that the actors make onstage.

The director and actor may consult you when they cannot remember what they did at the last rehearsal, and you will need to refer to the recorded blocking later when taking understudy rehearsals.

Blocking often has to be taken down at speed, sometimes while prompting at the same time. Always write in soft pencil; the moves will change several times before the first night. If you are forced to take it down quickly and roughly find time to tidy it up after the rehearsal. Use abbreviations and small diagrams.

Always use the character's name, not the actor's, and abbreviate it: for example Macheath becomes MAC.

Always use the same words and symbols for movements:

- Macheath crosses the stage: MAC X
- Macheath goes to...: MAC →
- Macheath comes on stage: MAC enters
- Macheath leaves the stage: MAC exits
- Macheath gets up: MAC rises.

Always be accurate and reasonably detailed. Specify *which* door or exit he is using; *which* chair he is sitting in.

Where there are several doors or chairs, number or label them and make a small sketch at the top of each page.

> MAC enters DOOR A
> and sits CHAIR 3

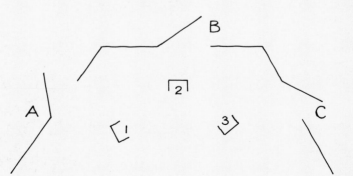

But how does he get to Chair 3? What path does he take when he crosses the stage? Does he move upstage or downstage, stage right or stage left? Each part of the stage has a name.

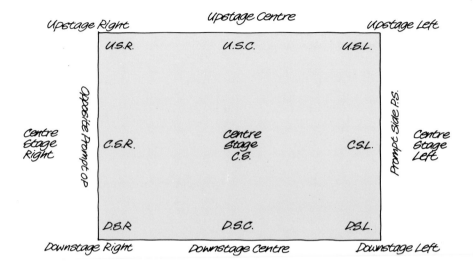

The next diagram shows a quick way of blocking, but the written version is more detailed.

MAC enters DOOR A X US of CHAIR 2 and SITS on DS arm of CHAIR 3 facing SR

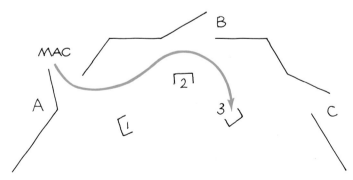

Every move should be *numbered* and written *opposite* its position in the script. Mark the exact point it happens in the script with a corresponding number.

ALTERNATIVE BLOCKING TECHNIQUES

If you are working with a non-proscenium arch stage discuss with your director how the acting area is to be labelled. To a certain extent any shaped space can be treated like a proscenium arch space, but here are two alternatives that might be suitable. Always sit in the same place for every rehearsal.

Promenade theatre (audience inside acting area)

MAC enters SW X to SSE
POLLY enters NW X to WEST
MAC X to EAST

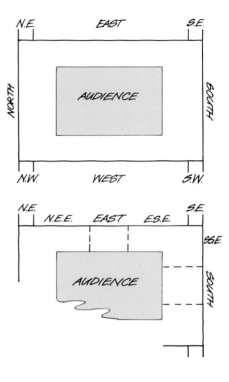

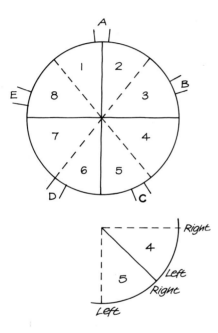

Theatre-in-the-round (audience outside)

MAC enters B X to middle of segment 7
POLLY enters F X to segment 5 left
MAC X to CS (segment 7)

CHOREOGRAPHY AND STAGE FIGHTS

Dance and fight notation is a specialized skill. See the chapters on musicals and stage fights.

CROWDS

It is impossible to record every movement of every person in a busy crowd scene. But you may want to split them into groups, label them and record their exits and entrances and main positions onstage at given moments.

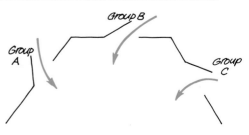

THE TEXT

Cuts and rewrites

The text in the prompt script has to be accurate. Make all cuts clearly, using straight lines in soft pencil. Insert and change words distinctly. If a large section of the script has been rewritten retype the whole page. If the rewritten section is only a few lines long then type the new text on a slip of paper and stick it on top of the old text.

Prompting

Always prompt in a strong, clear voice. Be sensitive to what is happening in the scene. Do not bellow a prompt in the middle of a quiet moment such as a love or death scene. Likewise, do not whisper a prompt in a noisy crowd scene!

Try to look up at the actors as often as possible while following the text with your hand. Some actors may ask for a prompt but some will not want to break out of character and may just look up in your direction. Every time there is a silence look up at the actors to see whether they are acting or whether someone has really dried. Mark all acting pauses in the script to remind yourself not to prompt at those moments.

Check with your director as to how accurately the actors are to stick to the script. In the early stages of rehearsal stop them and correct their mistakes. In the later stages, when the director wants the scene to flow on, make notes of their mistakes and inform them when it is over.

You may find yourself having to prompt and alter the blocking at the same time. If you have an ASM to help you, get them to prompt for you. Likewise, you may need to read in for missing actors – again this is where the ASM can help.

THE REST OF THE JOB

Be prepared to do anything and everything to make the rehearsal period comfortable, pleasant and efficient.

See that refreshments are always on hand. Encourage the company to make them for themselves.

Run errands in emergencies such as putting coins in parking meters; answer the telephone; take messages and make calls.

Act as an assistant to the director. You may be asked for advice on technical matters, or for your opinion on text interpretations and blocking problems. Get to know your director's particular needs.

Keep a note of the dates and times of the director's meetings, and remind him or her of things that need doing and questions that need asking. Stand in for missing actors while the director is trying to block a scene, especially if the actor uses props. Should the production require extras who cannot attend until the last moment, make a note of all they do and block them in yourself if the director does not have time.

Help the director with company discipline. A large cast can get very noisy. Speak in a loud, clear voice to gain their attention.

Be helpful to the acting company. Do not get involved in company disputes. Remain sympathetic to all, but as unbiased as possible.

Finally, try to maintain a sense of humour!

THE ASM (SECOND ASSISTANT) IN REHEARSAL

Learn the DSM's job. You may need to take over at short notice. Learn what needs to be done and do it without waiting to be asked – try to stay one jump ahead. Do anything that enables the DSM to stay on the book.

THE LONE STAGE MANAGER

If you are a stage manager without a team to back you up it hardly needs to be said that you must organize your time carefully. Set up the rehearsal room before the rehearsal and clear it up at the end, encouraging the acting company to lend a hand. Make sure you receive notes from the director after every rehearsal. Spend the rest of the time organizing and propping. Attend as many run-throughs as possible if you are going to cue or operate the lighting or sound in performance. Encourage the actors to take care of and set their own props if there is too much for one person to handle.

ALL: Thank you, sir. ①

② BROWN: I'm delighted to meet my old friend Mac's charming wife. ③

POLLY: Don't mention it, sir.

MAC: ~~Sit down,~~ You old bugger, ~~and~~ pitch into the whisky! — ④ Polly and gentlemen! You have today in your midst a man whom the king's inscrutable wisdom has placed high above his fellow men and who has none ~~the less~~ remained my friend throughout the storms ~~and~~ perils, and so on. You know who I mean, ~~and~~ you too know who I mean, Brown. Ah, Jackie, ~~do you remember how we served in India together, soldiers both of us?~~ Ah, Jackie, let's sing the Cannon Song right now. ⑤

~~They sit down on the table.~~

Song lighting: golden glow. ~~The organ is lit up. Three lamps are lowered from above on a pole, and the signs say:~~

THE CANNON SONG

⑥ John was all present and Jim was all there
⑦ And Georgie was up for promotion.
⑧ Not that the army gave a bugger who they were
When confronting some heathen commotion.
⑨ ⑩ The troops live under
The cannon's thunder
⑪ From the Cape to Cooch Behar.
⑫ Moving from place to place
When they come face to face
⑬ With a different breed of fellow
Whose skin is black or yellow
⑭ They quick as winking chop him into beefsteak
tartare.

⑰
⑮ Johnny found his whisky too warm
And Jim found the weather too balmy
⑯ But Georgie took them both by the arm
And said: never let down the army.
The troops live under
The cannon's thunder

CUES	BLOCKING
	1 Gang sit USR
	2 Brown x to DSC
	3 Mac x to US of table + pours whiskey into 2 glasses.
	4 Mac x to SR of Brown & gives him glass.
	5 Both drink
	6 Mac salutes
	7 Brown raises glass
	8 Both throw glasses over shoulders
	9 Both pretend to hold rifles on shoulders.
	10 Both march DSC
	11 Both paint DS on the beats
	12 Mac → SR Brown → SL
	13 Both turn DS
	14 Both make chopping motions on the beat
	17 Join CS + tango
	15 Mac → SR Brown → SL
	16 Both pretend to link arms

OUTSIDE THE REHEARSAL ROOM

During the rehearsal period the stage management team will be just as busy outside the rehearsal room as inside.

PRODUCTION MANAGEMENT

Having decided that it is possible to mount the production in terms of money, time and manpower it is the production manager who begins to set the wheels in motion. You should arrange meetings between the designer and carpenters who are to build the set; with the wardrobe personnel who are to make or acquire the costumes; and with the props department or stage management who will be making or finding the props, dressing and furniture. You must ensure that the designer is available to work closely with them during the coming weeks, and to pay regular visits yourself to all departments to ensure that everything is running smoothly.

PRODUCTION BUDGET

From the initial costings given by the technical departments you should be able to break down the budget into sections. Try to ensure that none of the groups exceeds its allocation.

Petty cash

You should always have a certain amount of cash available. Allocate a certain sum of petty cash per week to each head of department. In order to keep track of all the money you are handing out make everyone sign a petty cash receipt before they get it.

PRODUCTION BUDGET BREAKDOWN

THE THREEPENNY OPERA   BUDGET: 2,500

SHOW   Designer

Director   Stage Manager

Production Manager

SET	BUILDING	600
	PAINT/TEXTURE	100
	SCAFFOLDING HIRE	160
	WIRE NETTING	50
		———
	SET SUB TOTAL	950.00
LIGHTING	EQUIPMENT HIRE	200
	GEL/GOBOS/LAMPS	50
	EFFECTS	100
		———
	LX SUB TOTAL	350.00
SOUND	EQUIPMENT HIRE	100
	TAPE	10
	MICROPHONE HIRE	50
		———
	SOUND SUB TOTAL	160.00
WARDROBE	COSTUME HIRE	100
	MAKING	100
	BUY	200
	WIGS	50
	RUNNING COSTS	30
		———
	WARDROBE SUB TOTAL	460.00
	HIRE	100
		100

PRODUCTION MEETINGS

You should call a production meeting as soon as possible after rehearsals have begun. Those attending should include the director, designer, stage management and heads of all technical departments

At this point many of the people involved will only have seen the sketches or working drawings pertaining to themselves. This meeting allows the director and designer to present their production to the production team as a whole. It is essential that everyone feels that they are working together to the same end, so they all need to have an idea of what everyone else is contributing.

This meeting is also an opportunity for each department to discuss any problems they are having with the production, particularly financial ones. Should one department find that it needs more money it may be possible to reshuffle the budget, taking some from a department that thinks it can come in under budget. If this is not possible and the produc-

tion budget cannot be increased, then compromises have to be reached. It may be possible to achieve the same scenic effect by using cheaper methods and materials than those first suggested by the designer, or if not, then by adapting pieces that are in stock. You may have to persuade the director and designer to cut or alter things in order to save money.

During the rehearsal period you should call regular progress meetings to ensure that everyone is sticking to their budgets and staying on schedule.

It is essential for a PM (PSM) to have a good knowledge of building materials and methods, and of course prices. Build up a card index of local tradesmen – using the same suppliers over a period of time can sometimes win discounts. Organize the information on a dual cross-referencing system – one headed with the names of the tradesmen, the other with the names of the items you are trying to find.

PRODUCTION SCHEDULE

The PM (PSM) must also work out a production schedule. Once a date for the opening night has been fixed, estimate how much time the production will need actually on stage if it is to be ready in time. Ask:

■ how many dress rehearsals?
■ how long a technical rehearsal?
■ how much time to plot the lighting and sound?

■ how long to rig and focus the lighting equipment?
■ how long to paint and dress the set?
■ how long to fit up the set?

After discussion with the director and relevant technical departments you will have to balance their needs with the amount of time that is available in the venue (and/or how much time the group can afford if they are being charged for it.)

PRODUCTION SCHEDULE

PRODUCTION MANAGER:

SHOW: STAGE MANAGER:

VENUE:

DAY 1
0.00 AM   Unload van and get in
            Commence fit up - flooring and flying pieces
            LX and sound rig front of house
0.00 PM   LX and sound rig onstage

DAY 2
0.00 AM   Continue fit-up - platforms, scaffolding, flatage, trucks, revolves,
                                fixtures and fittings
0.00 PM   Complete fit-up
            Test special FX, motorized trucks, revolves, etc. Paint the stage

DAY 3
0.00 AM   Painting and texturing
            Masking in position
            (start fitting up seating if applicable)
0.00 PM   LX complete rig and focus

DAY 4
0.00 AM   Dress the set and place furniture
            Organize the wings - treads, get offs, quick change rooms
            Set the props
0.00 AM   Scene change rehearsal
0.00 PM   Plot sound levels
0.00 PM   Plot lighting

DAY 5
0.00 AM   Technical rehearsal
0.00   Break
0.00 PM   Continue technical rehearsal
0.00   Finish

DAY 6
0.00 AM   Technical work onstage
            - finish painting/dressing etc
0.00 AM   - LX re rig/re focus
0.00 PM.   Dress rehearsal

DAY 7
0.00 AM   Technical work onstage
                - LX re plotting
                - Final painting of stage
            (Finish fitting up seating)
0.00 PM   Notes and rehearsal onstage
0.00 PM   Opening Night

STAGE MANAGEMENT

Rehearsal notes

Throughout the rehearsal period the stage manager should liaise with both the rehearsal room and the technical departments. You should discuss the day's rehearsal note with the DSM (first assistant), then distribute copies to every department. Follow up each note, discussing it with the department concerned.

There may be times when the director and designer supply conflicting information. For example, one may say a certain prop should be one size, when the other has asked for it to be another. You should make sure they come together to discuss the problem and agree on an answer so that you can pass on accurate information. Pass on any problems you feel you cannot handle to the PM and get advice.

Meetings

The SM should make sure that the director meets with all technical departments – lighting designer, sound department and props department – to discuss ideas and needs. Encourage the director to formulate these ideas·as soon before the production week as possible to give the departments plenty of time to change things if necessary.

Liaise with the wardrobe department over costume fittings, and arrange for them to be done as near the rehearsal room as possible. Both director and designer will want to attend these fittings if they can. They may also want a costume parade during the production week. Check with the PM if it is possible to have it on the stage.

Research

The SM may need to arrange for the acting company to visit theatres, cinemas or other areas related to the production. The director may also ask you to find/borrow/hire books, films or slides and you will need to arrange the equipment and a place to show them. The stage management team should be encouraged to join the acting company on these occasions if at all possible.

Petty cash

The PM should issue you with a regular supply of petty cash. Always keep it separate from personal money, preferably in a lockable container. Issue it to members of the team as they require it. Always get the recipient to sign for it and encourage everyone to collect a receipt for everything they purchase.

Organizing the team

Arrange for the whole stage management team to meet together at regular intervals to discuss their progress and problems. An ideal time for this is just before or after the day's rehearsal – the director may then be free to answer any questions.

The SM should divide the work that needs to be done as evenly as possible between the people available. Do not try to do everything yourself, but do not sit back and let the ASM (second assistant) do everything. Set weekly goals for the team to ensure they do not fall behind and leave time to spare before the production week to deal with last-minute changes and additions.

PROPPING

The provisional prop and furniture lists are only a starting point, and must be continually renewed and updated. A list of set dressings should be compiled with the designer.

Props

This means all articles handled by the actors such as cups, umbrellas, books and so on.

Dressings

These are articles that are part of the set, and not usually handled by the actors – curtains, paintings, ornaments or cushions.

Furniture

This covers the sofas, chairs and tables, etc used in the action of the play.

APPROACHING THE LIST

Before trying to find a prop make sure you know exactly what you are looking for. Make the director and designer be precise about their requirements:

- what is it to be used for?
- what size should it be?
- what colour/texture should it be?
- what period – modern/antique etc.?
- what quality – old and battered or new and smart?
- how is it to be used – roughly or gently?

SOURCES

Use stock

First look at any stock you may have with the designer. Even if an article is not entirely suitable it could be adapted.

Make

The designer will have made working scale drawings of any special props and dressing he wants. In some cases the carpentry workshop may need to do the initial building, and the stage management then adds the finishing touches.

Borrow

Build up a good relationship with local shops, businesses and museums. If approached in the right way they will often lend or give things in return for a credit in the programme and/or complimentary tickets for a performance.

Hire

Hiring is an expensive way of propping, and should be done sparingly and for the shortest possible time.

Buy

Running props (that is consumables such as cigarettes and food) may need to be bought. (Some large chain stores will often give away food vouchers.) Any non-perishables that you are forced to buy should find their way into the props store for future use.

SOURCE SHEET					USED IN PRO
ITEM	NAME OF COMPANY	NAME OF CONTACT	PHONE NO.	ADDRESS	of
1. Polaroid Camera	Jones Camera Shop	Mr Hughes	345 7794	34 High Street	The Threep
2. 1 Film & 2 Flash cubes for above	same	-	-	-	same
3. Ironing board (wooden)	-	Mrs Harris	054 9566	26 High Road	same
4. 1 Carpet Bag	-	-	-	-	same

EFFECTS

Stage management is usually responsible for any special effects required. Some, such as smoke, dry ice, clouds, gobos, explosions or telephones that are electrically operated, will be procured by the electricians. Likewise with taped sound effects. But the rest, including rain falling, door bangs, doorbells, gunshots and so on must be prepared by the stage management team.

GENERAL RULES

The SM is in charge of the prop/furniture/dressing budget, so nothing should be bought or hired without your knowledge. The designer may wish to go on shopping/hire trips to choose everything personally, in which case a member of the SM team should go too. If the designer is unable to make visits to shops or hire firms a member of the team should take photographs of everything that appears suitable for the designer to choose from. Make sure everything is as authentic-looking and as accurate to the period as possible. Research into the style and period of the production thoroughly.

Let the director and actors rehearse with the real articles as soon as possible

Make sure both director and designer see and approve everything in plenty of time to change anything should it be necessary.

Do not put anything of great value on stage. If you have to, look into the possibility of insuring the object.

Keep a note of where everything has come from by making out source sheets.

Use source sheets to build up a card index of suppliers and sources so that the next time a similar prop is needed it can be found with the minimum amount of effort.

SHOW — THE THREEPENNY OPERA

DIRECTOR A.L.W.

DESIGNER S.C.

STAGE MANAGER D.H.

SHEET NO 1

PROP	Scene/Page No.	ADDITIONAL INFORMATION	POSSIBLE SOURCE
SWORD STICK	Scene 1 4	Ivory Tipped.	
LARGE SIGN	6	4ft x 4ft with 3ft long handle.	HIRE/BORROW MAKE
BIBLE	6	Large, Black, old and Battered.	STOCK
MAP OF CITY	7	3ft x 3ft - mounted on black board.	MAKE
Addition BLACKBOARD and EASEL BUSINESS CARDS	7	Jeremaiah V. Peachum 'THE BEGGAR'S FRIEND'.	MAKE
5 DUMMIES	8	Shop display dummies Clothed as beggars.	BORROW WARDROBE
COINS	8	10 silver shillings Peachum personal.	
PAPER MONEY	8	In thick wedge to look like old £1 notes	MAKE
CANDLEWAX Addition SWEET JAR	9	Shredded candle wax	BUY/MAKE
IRON	9 9	Old glass sweet jar. Old, battered- with lead non practical.	BORROW STOCK

BORROW/ HIRE ETC.

	BORROW/ HIRE ETC.
...era	Borrow
	Same
	Borrow
	Stock

STOCK

Your own stock of props and furniture, however small, can save you money. Even if it is not good enough to use on stage it will be suitable for use in rehearsal.

PROPS STORAGE

Store your stock carefully so that things do not get lost or broken, and always keep it tidy. Organize your stock so that things are easy to find, and always return everything to its proper place. Use boxes, shelves and stackable bins /racks, labelled according to their contents.

FURNITURE STORAGE

Space large enough to store furniture can be expensive and difficult to find. You may have to settle for storage that is some distance from the company's base, or disperse furniture through space volunteered by company members and others. The designer will need access to your stock, so to save time and travelling photograph everything you have and make up a stock book with the details of each piece. The designer can then judge the suitability of your stock with the minimum of effort.

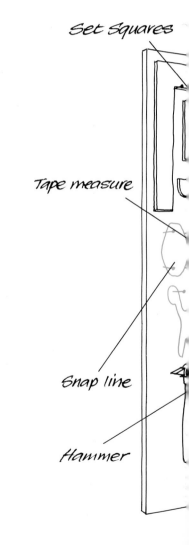

Set Squares

Tape measure

Snap line

Hammer

PROPS WORKSHOP

Prop making can be dirty and sometimes dangerous if the correct precautions are not taken. Materials such as glass fibre, spray paint, expanded foam, polystyrene, latex and some adhesives present their own particular problems. Always take notice of the directions and warnings on containers. Wear protective masks over eyes or mouth and gloves where necessary.

Keep a well-equipped first aid box easily accessible. Take care when using tools. Do not use damaged tools especially electrically operated ones and always use appropriate safety guards on machinery.

Store tools and materials away safely.

Allocate a workshop space, no matter how small, and divide it into areas. Ideally there should be separate areas for woodwork, sewing, paperwork, use of toxic substances and wet materials. Display no smoking signs and have the right kind of extinguishers to hand. Make sure toxic areas are well ventilated.

In addition there should be a separate area in which to keep finished props. In this way it is less likely for accidents to happen or props to be broken or spoiled.

This shadow board shows how tools may be stored safely.

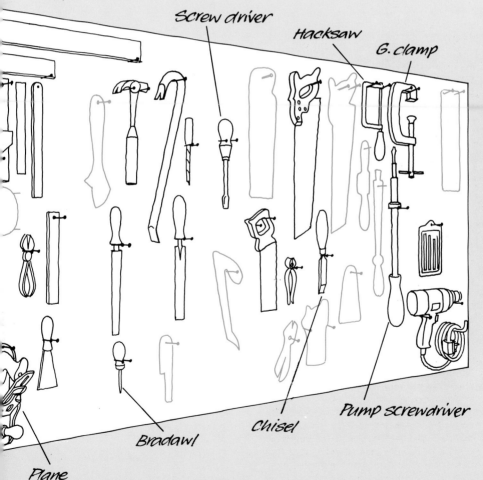

Screw driver

Hacksaw

G. clamp

Pump screwdriver

Chisel

Bradawl

Plane

CHAPTER 4

PREPARING FOR PRODUCTION WEEK

As production week draws near work intensifies and the stage management team must start pulling together all the various components and making plans for running the show.

INSIDE THE REHEARSAL ROOM: RUN-THROUGHS

All members of the stage management team who will be working on stage during the production should attend at least one run-through in the final week of rehearsal. As preparation they should take charge of the scene change and prop setting, using the lists prepared by the DSM (first assistant).

The DSM should take charge in the rehearsal room for a run-through in the same way that he or she will have to on stage. Make sure everyone is ready to begin, then ask them to stand by in their positions. Start the run by announcing curtain or lights up and do the same for each act/scene. Also time each act every time it is run.

If it is not possible to do a run on the set, or at least on stage, before the technical rehearsal it is up to the stage management team to provide as realistic a setting as possible in the rehearsal room.

The lighting designer, and possibly other members of the production team, will need to watch a run-through so they must be kept informed of when one is planned to take place.

PAPERWORK

Cue sheets and setting lists must be made for all the technical departments to use during the technical rehearsal:

- prop setting lists
- furniture setting list/diagram
- scene change lists/diagrams
- sound cue list
- fly cue list
- truck cue list
- slide cue list
- quick change list.

Make copies of all lists – enough for the SM and DSM and all relevant operators.

Lighting cues will be worked out by the lighting designer and director at the lighting plotting session.

GROUND PLAN

The final positions of furniture/scenic elements and all electrics/practicals should be marked on the ground plan (lamps, television/stereo systems and fires).

The set designer and heads of technical departments must be informed of any changes from the original plan and copies of the new plan made if necessary.

PROP SETTING LIST

SHOW   THE THREEPENNY OPERA

STAGE RIGHT

Prologue

1 Large green umbrella (Mr Peac

1 Red umbrella (Mrs Peachum)

1 Camera (Mrs Peachum)

1 Small pink umbrella (Polly)

6 Pieces of silk - 3 red (Begg

3 Yellow

1 Banner - God is Just (Begga

Scene 1

1 Iron & cloth (Mrs Peachum)

PROMPT SCRIPT

The positions of all known cues and cue numbers should be marked in the prompt script. The calls for actors and stage staff should also be put in before the technical rehearsal. This can be a time-consuming job, and should be dealt with before production week when time will be too short to do it.

MOVING OUT

The last rehearsal will usually take place just before the director and DSM (first assistant) are required at the performance venue, which will probably be for the lighting and sound plotting sessions.

Transport must be arranged to take everything to the venue in time for the lighting session. When packing up take care to separate rehearsal items from the actual items to be used on stage. Rehearsal items can then be returned to their storage places as soon as is convenient. Remove the mark-up tape from the floor and remember to leave the room clean and tidy.

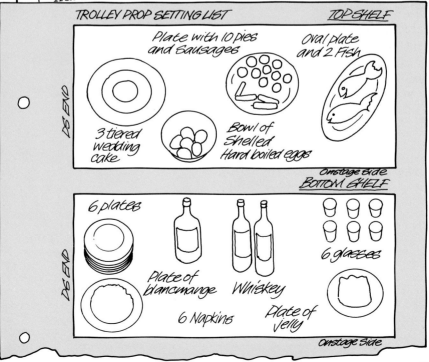

TROLLEY PROP SETTING LIST   TOP SHELF

Plate with 10 pies and sausages

Oval plate and 2 Fish

3 tiered wedding cake

Bowl of Shelled Hard boiled eggs

Onstage Side
BOTTOM SHELF

6 plates

6 glasses

Plate of blancmange

Whiskey

6 Napkins

Plate of Jelly

Onstage Side

THE THREEPENNY OPERA

SHOW

ON STAGE PRESET FOR ACT 1   (PROLOGUE)

Cardboard Boxes

7. Upturned chair - Chippendale

1. 5 Dummies joined

8. Mattress against wall on its side

2. Curtain on costume rail

9. Door - the same

3. Oil drum (upright)

10. Trolley and props (see setting list)

4. Oil drum (on its side)

11. Desk and Stool

5. Red/yellow carousel set upside down

6. 2 Tea chests

PROP SETTING LIST

THE THREEPENNY OPERA

SHEET NO 1 (of 1)

Show

PERSONAL PROPS

Mr Evans   Dressing room 1
(Macheath)

1 Swordstick
1 Wadge of £1 notes
6 Shilling pieces

1 Handbag: containing lipstick
and powder compact

Miss Gardener   Dressing room 2
(Polly)

1 Notebook and pencil
1 Police whistle

                 Dressing room 3

48

Knitting - 2 needles and b

SHOW   FLY CUES

DSM   THE THREEPENNY OPERA

PRESET

FOH TABS IN
U.S. SHUTTER - IN

FLUORESCENT LIGHTS - OUT

CUE 1

CUE 2   FOH TABS OUT - FAST

CUE 3   U.S. SHUTTER OUT TO MIDDLE DEAD - SLOW

CUE 4   U.S. SHUTTER OUT ALL THE WAY - SLOW

CUE 5   U.S. SHUTTER IN ALL THE WAY - FAST

FOH TABS IN - FAST

INTERVAL

CUE 6

FLUORESCENT LIGHTS - IN

ACT II

CUE 7

CUE 8   FOH TABS OUT - SLOW

CUE 8A   U.S. SHUTTER OUT ALL THE WAY - FAST

U.S. SHUTTER IN ALL THE WAY - SLOW

(POSSIBLY VISUAL AS ACTOR CLEARS)

QUICK CHANGES

SHOW   THE THREEPENNY OPERA

ACT/SC	PLACE	DETAILS
End of Prologue	S/L	Miss Garden out of beggar's costume into Polly
	S/R	Miss Shade and the Mr McFadder out of Beggars costume into Peachum
End of Sc 2	S/L	Miss Garden out of bridal costume into Polly very fast
End of Act II Sc 5	S/R	Miss Winter out of whore costume into Police Woman. Very fast

SOUND CUES

SOUND CUES

THE THREEPENNY OPERA

SHOW

DSM

CUE 1	VAN DRIVING UP AND STOPPING (US – LEFT SPEAKER)
CUE 2	ALARM BELL (ALL SPEAKERS)
CUE 2A	FADE ALARM BELL
CUE 3	MICROPHONE UP
CUE 4	MICROPHONE OUT
CUE 5	VOICES AND FOOTSTEPS (US – LEFT SPEAKER)
	BELLS

STAGE MANAGEMENT RUNNING PLOT AND LIVE FX LIST

SHOW   THE THREEPENNY OPERA

SHEET NO 1

1. At Beginners' Call	Smoke cue/cover stage with smoke before curtain goes up

2. Check Act 1 Beginners	S/R S/L ONSTAGE
	Mr Evans Miss ... Miss ...
	  Mr ... Miss ...
	  Mr ... Miss ...
	   Mr ...
	   Mr ...

3. Prologue	Top up smoke onstage during Prologue
4. Act 1 (finale)	Smoke cue
5. Check Act 11 Beginners	S/R S/L ONSTAGE Miss ... Miss ... Miss ... Mr ... Mr ... Mr ...
6. Act 11 Sc 5 p.60	3 loud door knocks from USL On cue light

OUTSIDE THE REHEARSAL ROOM

Liaison with technical departments

The production manager is responsible for liaison with all departments to ensure that everything will be ready in time, and to discuss any last-minute problems. You should find out how many staff each will need for the get-in (load-in), fit-up (put-in) and running the show. Also find out what equipment and materials they will need, and arrange for them to be available at the theatre – extra lanterns (lamps) and cable, costume rails and washing machine, tools and hardware, paint and texturing materials. You should call a technical planning meeting to discuss the final production schedule and allocation of stage time and any final adjustments to the ground plan. This will give the chief electrician (and lighting designer if available), master carpenter and stage manager (plus designer, if available) an opportunity to discuss the fit-up and any problems that may arise such as the division of flying bars between pieces of scenery and lighting equipment.

Liaison with venue

The PM must also check that the production schedule is acceptable to the venue's personnel. Arrange for the appropriate number of stage, electrics and wardrobe staff to be available. Check the venue facilities: number of dressing rooms, laundry and other equipment available. Ensure that any theatre stock you are planning to use will be suitable and available, for example stock rostra (platforms), door boxes, treads, curtains and masking, and if not, make provision to acquire what you need from other sources. Also check there is adequate access to the stage, and that your set is not too large to fit through the doors. Also check that there is adequate parking space nearby and that your transport will have no problems gaining access.

If the venue does not have a fixed auditorium, arrangements will have to be made to create one. If the venue provides its own seating and/or rostra, directions must be given as to how and when it is to be set up. The PM may have to make arrangements to hire or borrow seating or rostra if the venue does not supply them.

Safety and fire regulations must be adhered to when creating an auditorium. Seats must be attached and adequate space left between rows and fire exits. Battens should be fixed to the edges of rostra, and steps may be needed to gain access to high rostra or scaffolding levels. Hand rails may be needed if the steps are at all steep, and a line of white tape or paint should be put along all rostra edges.

TRANSPORT

The set, props, costumes, tools and equipment will all need to be transported to the theatre, and boxes or lockable containers should be made available for packing.

STAGE MANAGEMENT PREPARATIONS

The stage management team must make sure that all the props are ready for the technical rehearsal and that they have all been approved by both the director and designer. Furniture and any scenic elements made by the props department must be ready for the lighting session.

The team will be helping the designer to dress the set, so all items of dressing must be ready before the lighting session. Curtains must be made and rails ready to go up, and picture hooks, door furniture and any other fixings bought.

Any special effects should be tried and tested before moving into the venue.

The director and lighting designer must be brought together to discuss the lighting and arrangements made for the lighting designer to see a run-through.

The director should also listen to the sound tape in plenty of time for adjustments to be made before the sound plotting session.

The wardrobe department should be consulted over the number of dressers required, if any, and whether a quick change room will be needed on stage. Dressing rooms should be allocated with advice from the wardrobe department and a list should be made ready to post at the stage door. Labels bearing the names of the actors should be made ready to be placed on each dressing room door.

The SM and DSM must also decide how the show is to be cued, that is, which department will use cue lights and which headsets (cans). If the equipment is not available in the theatre, provision must be made to acquire it and have it installed by the electrics department.

Transport must also be arranged to pick up hired or borrowed items and transport them to the venue.

A list of credits must be given to the administrator or whoever is arranging the programme. Anyone who has lent or given anything to the production should be mentioned and any complimentary tickets promised must be sent to the people concerned or arrangements made to leave them at the box office.

THE STAGE

Any type of stage can be a dangerous place to work if proper precautions and procedures are not adhered to. Always keep it tidy, well organised, and free from extraneous objects.

STOCK SCENERY

Storage space is a good idea so as to build up a stock of basic scenery that can be adapted for use as necessary. This could save a great deal of time and money.
Stock should include:

■ door and window boxes
■ fireplaces
■ rostra (platforms)
■ flats
■ treads
■ floorcloths.

As with furniture a scenic store of any size benefits from a cataloguing system. Show the designer a photograph before pulling large items out of a crowded store. Number and measure flats, rostra and such like, and enter details in a stock book.

MASKING

Most venues will have their own stock of masking but it is a good idea to build up your own, especially if touring:

■ masking flat: flat covered in canvas painted black or black serge (velour)
■ backing flat: part of the scenic design used behind doors or windows
■ book flats (ballet masking): two flats hinged together and set at right angles to each other (usually used on an open stage design)
■ legs: lengths of black material hung vertically from the end of flying bars
■ borders: long thin lengths of black material hung horizontally from flying bars to mask the grid or lighting bars.
■ hard borders: long thin lengths of covered flatage used in the same way.

Soft masking can be made to look hard by inserting metal rods in the hems to stretch them out. Legs can be anchored to the stage with the aid of stage weights or wooden battens nailed to the floor. Flats should be secured with braces or hinged to the floor, and tied off to the rail of the fly floor.

BASIC STAGE EQUIPMENT

To join flatage together
hinges
pin hinges and hinge pins
sash cord
tie off and throw line cleats
battens

To hold flatage up
extending braces and screw eyes
french braces
stage weights
stage screws

To gain access
straight and A-frame ladders

To keep the stage clean
stage brooms
mops and buckets
brush and pan

TOOLS AND HARDWARE

Selection of:
hammers
saws
screwdrivers
electric drill
staple gun
tape measure
chalk line
coloured plastic tapes.

set squares
chisels
file
bradawls
mallet
wire cutters
scissors

plane
G-clamps
torch
spanners
scale rule
wing bolts

screws
nails
trimming knife
spirit level

THE FLYS

Every venue and theatre varies in its capacity for flying scenery. Some may have a sophisticated counterweight system, others a basic manual hemp line system. Some may have no room over the stage or equipment to fly at all. Venues that do have some kind of flying system should have a selection of stock drapes and masking available and someone who can supervise the use of the equipment.

Stock

Basic stock will probably include:

> Front-of-house curtains (tabs)
> Set of black serge curtains
> Borders and soft legs
> Painted cloths
> Black gauze
> Projection screen
> Curtain track

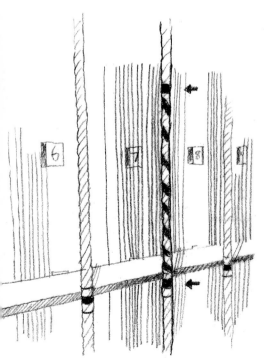

Stock should be stored in clean, labelled bags. Curtains and cloths should be folded neatly with the DS side inwards and ties easily accessible. Measure all curtains and legs, and enter details in a stock book.

Hanging

Basic equipment for venue with a flying system:

> Flying wire or hemp rope
> Flying irons, grummets and wire grips
> Sand bags, cleats and pulleys

Hang masking and scenic pieces as marked on the ground plan and made up in a hanging plot.

If the venue has no flying facilities cloths and curtains can be attached to wooden battens and hung from the ceiling. A cloth that needs to move up and down can be tumbled or rolled up inside itself with the aid of ropes until it is out of sight of the audience, then unrolled downwards again when next needed.

Deading

Before using a flying piece in production it has to be decided how far in (down) and how far out (up) it is going to fly. These positions must be marked on the flying ropes or hemps.

The most outward position (nearest the grid) should always be marked in the same colour on each bar to ensure that the flyman does not fly them out too far, too fast and cause them to crash into the top of the theatre. During a show a bar needs to be flow out only far enough so that it is hidden behind the prosecenium arch or a border, out of sight of the audience. The SM should sit in the front row of the stalls and check that no flying pieces are visible.

Each dead should be preceded by a spiral of tape to warn the flyman to slow down and so decrease the risk of the flying piece bouncing on the stage floor.

THE FLY FLOOR

As with the stage floor it is essential for the fly floor (whether it be counterweight or hemp) and the loading gallery to be well organized and tidy. An object kicked or dropped accidentally from either could be lethal. It is advisable to lay carpet along the floor to cut down the possibility of the flyman being heard by the audience. This should be firmly fixed so there is no possibility of it being tripped over, and adequate working light provided. It may also be necessary to mask off the fly floor.

Flying

The flying crew should use the list of cues provided by the stage management, make any adjustments to it during the technical rehearsal, then make out a fly cue sheet.

The safest and most effective way to be cued when flying is to take the standby call over the headset, take off the headset and check the cue on the cue sheet. Go to the bar to be flown, wait for a red cue light, then take the brake off. Perform the cue when the green light comes on.

Head sets should not be worn when flying unless a safe and tidy system of extending the cable can be installed. The advantage of wearing a head set when flying is that stage management can stop a bar moving in case of emergency and give the flyman new instructions.

Safety rules

■ never fly a bar without first shouting a warning to the stage below. Show conditions are of course the exception

■ during scene changes when flying without a cue from the prompt corner, never fly a bar without first gaining clearance from the stage manager below

■ never drop anything from the fly floor without warning the stage below, for example 'Heads, upstage right.'

■ should a bar go out of control and the rope slip through your hands never try to keep hold it it unless you are wearing flying gloves.

HANGING PLOT

THEATRE
SHOW ___ THE THREEPEN

20	
19	UPSTAGE
18	
17	LX BAR
16	
15	LX BAR
14	
13	LX BA
12	
11	
10	
9	
8	LX
7	
6	
5	L
4	
3	
2	
1	

Flys Cue Sheet

SHOW: THE THREEPENNY OPERA

SHEET NO 1

CUE NO.	OPERATOR	ACTION	DEAD	REMARKS
PRESET				
		FOH TABS IN (BAR 1)		
		US SHUTTER IN (BAR 19) FLUORESCENTS OUT (15)		
1	A	FOH TABS OUT (BAR 1)		
2	B	US SHUTTER OUT (BAR 19)	BLUE	FAST
3	B	US SHUTTER OUT (BAR 19)	WHITE	SLOW
4	B	US SHUTTER IN (19)	GREEN	SLOW
		INTERVAL	BLUE	FAST
6	A	FLUORESCENTS IN (BAR 15)	BLUE	INTERVAL CHANGE
7	B	FOH TABS OUT (BAR 1)	BLUE	SLOW
8	A	US SHUTTER OUT (BAR 19)	GREEN	FAST
8a.	A	US SHUTTER IN	BLUE	CUE FROM O.P.B. WHEN ACTOR CLEAR - SLOW

55

HEALTH AND SAFETY ON STAGE

Dressing for the job
Overalls or a boiler suit
Strong shoes
Hard hat (optional)
Goggles (if welding)
Mask (when using toxic substances)
Tool belt

General safety rules
■ never try to lift anything too large by yourself
■ never leave tools at the top of a ladder unattended
■ never climb ladders with tools in your pockets. Invest in a tool belt
■ never climb a ladder without someone at the foot to hold it steady and stop it slipping
■ never step over flying bars; they should be worked on at chest height
■ never leave pieces of wood with nails or screws sticking out on the stage floor
■ never leave lifts or traps open and unattended
■ do not smoke on stage
■ do not bring food or drink on to the set (other than props)
■ mark the edges of get-offs (steps) and rostra (platforms) with a line of white tape or paint
■ secure masking both at stage level and at the top
■ always give the acting company a tour of the set and backstage areas before the technical rehearsal, pointing out any danger points.

When organizing the wings consider all the following safety precautions:

■ do not obscure fire exits and access points to an electrics perch or fly floor
■ keep the wings tidy, clean and free of anything not related to the show
■ secure any flats or ladders stored there
■ provide adequate blue working lights for show conditions
■ tape down any cable to the floor
■ put down carpet runners and secure with tape

■ paint stage weights and braces white or distinguish with lengths of white tape
■ secure any overhead ropes or cables above head height or mark them clearly.

FIRST AID

Keep a well-stocked first-aid box near the stage and make sure everyone knows where it is.
Know where the nearest hospital with an accident department is.
Make sure that whenever possible there is someone trained in first aid available in the theatre.

FIRE REGULATIONS

Enforce the no-smoking rule backstage and display signs. Work out a backstage fire drill and display directions in all areas. Hold regular fire drill practices.
Create a fire code word.
Make sure that all fire exits, backstage or in the auditorium, are clearly marked and not blocked. Adequate space between rows of seating should be left to enable the audience to exit speedily in case of fire.
Some local fire stations will not allow naked flames or any non-fireproofed materials on stage. Make sure you know how stringently these rules are upheld in the venue. Your set and props may need to be made from fire-resistant materials or be fireproofed before opening night.

Fireproofing
Flame-resistant materials are available, but are of course more expensive than other kinds. If the run is to be short, fireproofing the set and props after they are made will be cheaper. Fireproofing and fire-retardant substances are available in solution or crystal forms. Articles can be dipped, painted or sprayed.

Naked flames
Prop battery-operated candles and torches are available or can be made if naked flames are not allowed. If a naked flame is to be used make sure that it is moved about on stage as little as possible. Torches, braziers or containers should be made of metal or non-combustible materials and a paraffin

wax candle used to make the flame.

If the container has to be moved the candle must be securely fixed, covered with a wire mesh and easy to extinguish. Always have a fire extinguisher/sand bucket standing ready in the wings. Put ashtrays containing water or sand on the prop tables for extinguishing cigarettes and cigars.

Pyrotechnics

Most flash pots and maroons (firecrackers) are electrically operated, but it is often the stage management team who have to set them off. Always follow the directions to the letter. Never fire any pryotechnics closer than the prescribed distance. Always use a bomb tank where specified. This can be made from a strong metal dustbin with a medium-mesh wire cover securely fixed over it.

Fire-Fighting equipment

Many theatres have an iron curtain and a water drencher system. The curtain should be lowered in the intermission and raised again for the second half. All backstage areas and workshops should be well supplied with extinguishers, fire buckets, sand buckets, and fire blankets. There are several different kinds of fire extinguisher, suitable for use on different types of fire.

Make sure equipment is checked regularly.

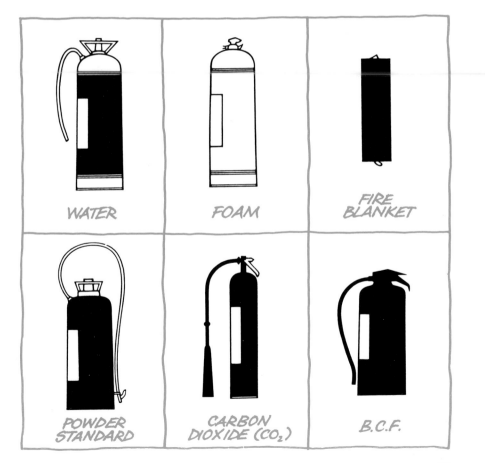

WATER

FOAM

FIRE BLANKET

POWDER STANDARD

CARBON DIOXIDE (CO_2)

B.C.F.

THE PRODUCTION WEEK

The production week should proceed as set out in the production schedule and be overseen at all times by the production manager. The person in charge of each section runs their part of the proceedings and the stage manager should ensure that everything is coming together in the way the director and designer intended.

THE GET-IN (LOAD-IN)

First clear and tidy the stage ready for the incoming production, leaving the maximum space available for the set and equipment. Each part of the set should be clearly marked so that it can be stacked in the most convenient positions on stage as it comes off the lorry. Stage left and stage right sections and flying pieces should be separated. Electrical equipment, costumes, props, and furniture should be stored separately away from the main fit-up area until needed.

THE FIT-UP (LOAD-IN)

1 Mark out the stage as shown on the groundplan.
2 Hang all flying pieces, curtains and cloths.
3 Lay down the stage cloth or other floor covering. (If the set prevents flying bars being lowered to working height some preliminary lighting rigging may need to be scheduled in. If the stage is to be heavily raked or built up to different levels the electricians may also need to focus some of the lanterns.
4 Build up the rake or set up rostra (platforms) or scaffolding.
5 Fit up main parts of the set.
6 Main lighting and sound rigging session.
7 Paint and texture the set.
8 Put the masking in place and 'dead' the flying bars. (Make sure the electricians will have enough space to bring ladders and other access equipment on to the stage.) Put in get-offs (steps) and mark their edges with white tape.
9 Check the sight lines. The audience should not be able to see any equipment or parts of the stage that the director and designer had not intended. Sit in the middle of the front row and check that the bottoms of flying pieces, bars or electrics equipment are never visible. Adjust the borders and out-deads of flying pieces until the upper parts of the stage are masked.
Sit at either end of the front row and make sure neither the wings nor fly floors are

visible. Sit at the back of the circle or gallery and check that the audience will not be able to see over the back of the set.

Mark the sight line on the stage floor behind each masking flat, door and window, with a line of white tape, to ensure that no one accidentally walks into the audience's line of vision during performances.

10 In the case of an acting space without a fixed auditorium, where seating rostra and chairs have to be used, it is essential to mark out the extremities of the seating at this stage. Mark the front row and the ends of the rows in order to check sight lines and to give the electricians a guide to the limits of the acting space when focusing and plotting. The seating could be set out at this stage provided that there is no lighting equipment hanging above the area that the electricians will need access to.

11 Lighting focusing session. Stage management should mark the position of practical lighting on the stage and the positon of the front of seating where applicable.

DRESSING THE SET

The SM team should be prepared to assist the designer dress the set. Once ornaments, plants, pictures and furniture have been placed on the set and their positions agreed, these must be documented and marked on the stage or set.

Furniture positions should be marked on the floor using a different colour tape for each scene. Plants, ornaments and pictures should be numbered and labelled and a corresponding label put on to the stage floor or set wall. A detailed drawing should be made showing how everything is positioned and if possible a photograph taken of each set. In this way you can ensure the scene is set up correctly after every scene change and in every new venue. Any items on stage that do not need to be moved during the course of the play should be securely fixed down to prevent breakages. Use clear sticky tape or re-usable adhesive to secure lids on jars or pots, and glass shades on oil lamps or similar. Use wire or nylon fishing line to tie down plants, vases, and ornaments. Tape down wires and cables to practical lamps or telephones, and put double-sided tape under carpets and mats to prevent slipping.

SETTING THE PROPS

Set up prop tables in the wings where they are easily accessible but not in the way of scene changes and fire exits. Using the DSMs setting lists, set the props on the side of the stage from where the actors using them make their entrances. Make a list of personal props, such as watches, spectacles and so on, and check these before every performance. If your acting space does not have actual wing areas check with the director and designer as to whether they want the prop tables visible to the audience or not.

Try to keep props on, under or beside the prop tables and preferably against a wall to avoid obstructing exits and entrances. Paint the tops of the tables black and mark out a grid using white tape. Put a prop in each section and write the name of it on the tape below. Do the same on the wall beside the tables for large props. Display a checklist above each table.

If there is not enough space to set out all the props from the start, then reset the table during the intermission. Instead of marking out the tables cover them with large sheets of strong paper or card and mark them out instead. Use a different sheet for each act/part. After setting up the positions of furniture, dressing and props must be checked before every performance. The most effective way is to do a 'shout check'. This takes two people: one reads each prop from the list, the second checks its position, then the first ticks it off the list. Everything should also be checked for signs of wear and tear or damage. Unless otherwise specified by the designer, furniture should be dusted and polished regularly and all surfaces cleaned. Do not forget to check under tables and chairs as the audience in the front row may be able to see more than you imagine.

If the actors are required to eat and drink onstage take care to clean all utensils thoroughly and keep food fresh. Make tea and coffee fresh for every performance, and never use real alcohol; fruit juices and food colouring in water are preferable. Check with the actors concerned that they are not allergic to any particular foods and never vary the appearance or taste of food without warning them.

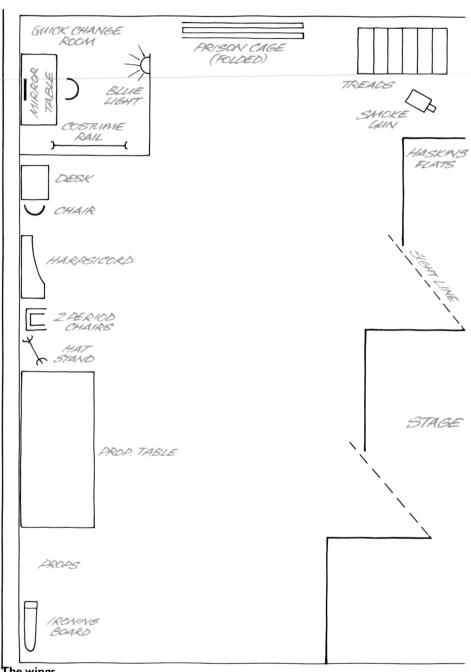

The wings

Organize the wings paying attention to the safey rules set out on page 56. Place furniture and scenery in the most convenient of positions for scene changes. Set up any quick-change rooms required and set up prop tables.

SCENE CHANGES

The stage manager should prepare the scene changes using the scene-change lists and diagrams produced by the DSM. All scene changes should be well organized and be done as quickly and efficiently as safety allows, whether they are concealed or in view of the audience. If they are to be done in front of the audience they should be choreographed with the crew wearing costume or black clothing and soft shoes.

The stage manager should establish how much time and how much light there will be to perform the change and whether the director would like the change performed in a black-out or in a special scene-change light. The SM should test how many people will be needed to move furniture safely. The changes can then be worked out on paper.

Scene change rehearsals

The director may want to organize the scene changes himself if they are to be performed in a particular style and/or using actors. But whether it is the stage manager or the director who directs the changes, a scene-change rehearsal should be called before the technical rehearsal, especially if the changes are numerous and complicated. Positions of furniture and dressing sometimes change during the lighting plotting sessions, so the ideal time for a scene-change rehearsal is between the plotting session and the technical rehearsal. Each member of the crew should receive a copy of the scene-change lists and diagrams with their particular part marked on them. The stage manager should allocate offstage effects operators in the same way.

Scene changes in performance

No member of the crew should ever run during a scene change, but walk at a brisk steady pace. They should practise aiming for the marks on stage and place the piece of furniture correctly at the first try, not shuffle it about. The stage should never be empty during the change and no one should stand about doing nothing. The crew should work on one side of the stage or the other as far as possible, making entrances and exits from the same side, so they do not have to cross the stage empty handed.

If any flying pieces have to move in or out during the scene change the stage manager should ensure that it is safe to do so and signal the flyman from the stage or cue him over the head set system. In some cases the DSM can cue the flys during scene changes provided he can see that it is safe. Once a scene change is complete the SM should give clearance to the DSM to continue to the next scene.

Props changes

It is advisable to allocate prop change to the ASMs during scene changes. When moving several small props on and off stage use trays to carry them. A very large number of props on a table can be moved most quickly by using a false table top.

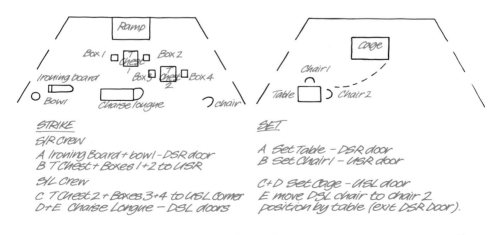

STRIKE

S/R Crew
A Ironing Board + bowl - DSR door
B T Chest + Boxes 1 + 2 to USR
S/L Crew
C T Chest 2 + Boxes 3 + 4 to USL corner
D + E Chaise Longue - DSL doors

SET

A Set Table - DSR door
B Set Chair 1 - USR door

C + D Set Cage - USL door
E move DSL chair to chair 2
position by table (exit DSR Door).

THE LIGHTING SESSION

The lighting (LX) plotting session is the time when the DSM should ensure that all the cues are in the prompt script. The director and lighting designer will plot the lighting cues in detail and the DSM should stay with them to ensure the positions and numbers of the cues are correctly noted. (If this is not possible the DSM should make sure to get the details of the cues from the lighting designer before the technical rehearsal.) The DSM should use this opportunity to finalize cueing sequences with help from the director, slotting in flying cues, truck cues and so on and marking in the positions of standbys.

The SM with an adequate number of stage staff should set up each scene in turn so that it can be lit. Positions of furniture and dressing may be adjusted by the director and designer. New positions should be marked and any changes noted on the scene-change lists.

Where there is no fixed auditorium as much of the seating as possible should be put in place for this session and for subsequent rehearsals.

Stage management personnel or stage staff should be available during the session to 'walk' on stage so that the director and lighting designer can see the effect the lighting will have on the actors.

SOUND PLOTTING SESSION

If a production has a large number of recorded sound effects or is to use microphones it is advisable to schedule a session to plot the sound levels. The DSM can then finalize the positions and numbers of the sound cues while the director and sound operator plot the levels.

COSTUME PARADE

The director and designer may want to see all the actors in costume on the stage before the technical rehearsal. A member of the stage management team should stay on stage to organize this and ensure that the actors arrive on stage in the prescribed order and that as little time as possible is wasted waiting for the next actor to arrive.

TECHNICAL REHEARSAL

Everything should be ready, available and working for this rehearsal. This is the time for the technical and backstage staff to rehearse their part in the production and for the actors to get used to the stage, set and props.

The production manager should sit with the director and designer to help with any problems that may arise. The stage manager should be in charge backstage to oversee the scene changes and offstage effects. If there is a problem the SM should stop the rehearsal, tell the director of the problem, put it right, then inform the DSM when ready so that the rehearsal can continue. Whenever the director stops the rehearsal the stage manager should appear on stage to assist if needed.

The ASMs should organize the props and assist the actors with their problems. If numbers allow there should be one on each side of the stage in charge of everything that happens in that wing. The ASMs should be prepared to take prop notes during the rehearsal and be available to help reset props and furniture whenever the director or stage manager wishes to go back to repeat a scene or part of the 'action'. The DSM should cue the production as set out in the prompt script. If she encounters problems she should stop the rehearsal and discuss the problems with the director if a quick solution cannot be found. When restarting the rehearsal she should ask where the director wants to start from and give the actors a line. If a cueing sequence or a scene change is to be repeated the DSM should ensure that the stage manager is ready, tell the operators where to set back to and put them on standby for the next set of cues. Then she should choose a place that is a few lines before the cues should happen and give the actors the appropriate line to start from. The actors may require a prompt during the technical rehearsal. This can be difficult for the DSM to do if involved with the cues and she should only prompt when free to.

The DSM must be prepared to make alterations to the prompt script. The director may wish to change, cut or add cues as the rehearsal progresses. The DSM should take down the alterations as quickly and clearly as possible.

Technical rehearsals are often long and always hard work. They require a great deal of concentration and patience from all concerned. It is essential to take regular sche- duled breaks even if the rehearsal is falling behind. Where time is short it may be possible to cut from cue to cue. If the director is willing, most of the dialogue between cues could be omitted to ensure that all the technical aspects of the production will have been rehearsed before the dress rehearsal.

PROMPT CORNER

If the show is a particularly straightforward one with very few cues, and technical personnel are few, it is possible for operators to have their own scripts with their cues marked in them, and/or stage management to operate sound and lights. There should be someone in the wings to prompt, though, and a member of stage management in charge backstage. There should also be some kind of telephone communication between the stage and the control positions. But if money and people allow, it is far preferable to have the member of stage management who has been in rehearsal (that is the DSM) in the prompt corner, prompting and giving all the cues to the technical departments.

Should it not be possible to position the cue desk so that the DSM can see enough of the stage, a video camera could be set up in the auditorium connected to a monitor in the prompt corner. Likewise, if the DSM is unable to hear enough of the play – for example if positioned in a sealed control room – a microphone could be set up near the stage connected to an amplifier and speaker in the control room.

CUEING

This can be done orally, with head sets, or visually, with cue lights. Either or both systems can be used.

HEAD SETS

It is essential when using a head set system to give cues to keep extraneous talking to the minimum. It is extremely difficult for the DSM (first assistant) to concentrate on what is happening on stage if operators are chattering over the communication system. During the technical rehearsal it is particularly difficult if the lighting designer is talking as well. If the lighting designer is still replotting with the board operator when the DSM needs to give cues the DSM should warn them that they should be on stand-by. The lighting designer will either require the DSM to stop the rehearsal until replotting is complete or stop replotting so that the DSM can continue.

Cues should be spoken clearly and quietly, not whispered. The stage manager or director should check that they cannot be heard in the auditorium.

Stand-bys should be given about half a page of standard text in advance. Take into account what the operators have to do before they are ready to do the cue. A computer lighting board operator who has only one button to press needs less warning than a manual board operator.

All operators should acknowledge the stand-by so that the DSM knows they are ready. When putting several operators on stand-by at once the DSM should wait for each one to acknowledge before going on to the next. But in a very busy production where cues are close together there may not always be time to wait for this.

Write the stand-bys (ST BYs) like this:

■ ST BY LX Qs 5-7: Say 'Stand by elecs cues five, six and seven.' (Response 'Standing by')
■ ST BY SOUND Qs 4-6: Say 'Stand by sound cues four, five and six.' (Response 'Standing by')
■ ST BY TRUCK Q 2: Say 'Stand by truck cue two.' (Response 'Standing by')

■ ST BY SLIDE Qs 3 + 4: Say 'Stand by slide cues three and four.' (Response 'Standing by').

If time is short run them all together and do not wait for a response. Just say:

■ 'Stand by elecs cues five to seven, sound cues four to six, truck cue two and slide cues three and four.'

When giving the cue try not to leave too much of a gap before the GO, but do not say the cue so fast that the operator is taken by surprise. Always think ahead. If there are several cues to give at the same time the DSM will have to start saying them several moments before the GO should happen. Find the optimum place to start saying the cue and mark it in the script.

When cueing several departments simultaneously write the cues one under another, bracket them together and write one go only. Say:

■ 'Elecs cue five, sound cue four, truck cue two and slide cue three: GO!'

CUE LIGHTS

Before the technical rehearsal the DSM should check which switch on the cue desk operates the cue light for which department. Label them accordingly.

Switch the red light on to put the operator on stand-by. Shorter stand-bys should be used for cue lights as it is very difficult to watch a light for too long without being distracted. Some cue lights have acknowledge buttons which either flash the red light or turn it off to tell the DSM that the light has been seen. When putting a department on stand-by for several cues in a sequence it is important to leave the red light on until the last cue has been given. It is just as important to turn the red light off promptly after the last cue has been taken.

When cueing with lights only, it is possible to ensure you do not turn the red light off too soon by drawing a vertical line from the stand-by down through all the cues, so joining them and stopping at the last cue in the sequence. Use a different colour for each department.

Use the green light to give the GO. Check that the cue is happening before turning it off. If a green light flashes on and off too quickly the operator may miss it. Likewise, it is just as important not to leave the light on too long as this may confuse the operator and could prove disastrous if it is still on when you next put on the red light.

USING BOTH SYSTEMS

The DSM may need to use head sets for some departments and cue lights for others. When writing out the cues make it clear which are to be given on cue lights and do not speak those cues over the headset. For example write stand-bys like this.

- LX Qs 1-6
- SOUND Qs 1-4
- STAGE RIGHT Q Light
- STAGE LEFT Q Light

When cueing the flys it is safer to use both systems as flying wearing a head set is not always safe. Put flys on stand-by over the head set at the same time as the rest of the departments in the cueing sequence. Then a few seconds before the cue (long enough for the flyman to take the brake off or un-cleat a hemp line) put the red cue light on. Then use the green light to give the cue.

FOLLOW-ON AND VISUAL CUES

It may not be possible for the DSM (first assistant) to give every cue. Sometimes they run so close together that there simply is not time. Operators can take a cue as a follow-on from the previous cue. The lighting designer will probably ask the board operator to take down the preset as soon as he has taken down the houselights. So the preset is a follow-on from the houselights. The DSM should ask the board operator to stand by for the houselights and follow-on, then give the go for the houselights, but not cue the follow-on.

Sometimes the operator may be able to see better than the DSM when to do the cue, particularly in the case of an actor turning on a light at a light switch. The board operator should take this as a visual cue. Again the

DSM should give a stand-by for the cue, with as reminder that it is a visual one, but should not then cue the operator to do it.

GENERAL RULES FOR THE DSM

Always check that cues have happened the way they should. It is essential that the prompt script contains information about what should happen when the cue is given as well as the cues themselves.

If a cue goes wrong you must know what has happened as it may effect other cues, or the action on stage. Stay calm in emergencies and talk the operator out of the problem. You should know what is best for the production, and must decide whether it is better to play a scene in the wrong lighting state or without a flying piece, rather than correct mistakes once the scene has started, so alerting the audience that something has gone wrong.

Indicate clearly in the prompt script exactly where and when each cue is to happen. If the cue happens on a word, draw a line from the cue to the word in the script. If the cue happens on a movement or on the completion of another cue indicate this in your cue column. (See overleaf.)

Everything should be written in pencil in the early stages as cues and their positions may change several times.

The person in charge of the prompt corner has an enormous responsibility. Wrongly or insensitively given cues can ruin a performance. You must know exactly what the director wants the audience to see and feel, and should use all your sensitivity to time cues so as to create the required effect.

CALLS

Call boys

If there is no public address system, back-stage calls should be made by one or more people running between dressing rooms. The DSM should write out the calls and number them. The call people should sit with the DSM who can then send them to make the appropriate call at the right time.

Public address system

Always test any system before using it, to discover the sensitivity of the microphone and the optimum amount of voice needed to use it. Work out exactly what to say before speaking into the microphone. Write out all calls in full and read them out if in doubt. Speak clearly and at a reasonable pace and always sound calm and collected. Repeat your message to ensure that it has been heard.

Where there is no show relay system it is essential to call actors for their entrances. Call them about two pages of average dialogue before their entrance, to give them enough time to adjust their costume and make-up, to find their props and prepare their concentration. (The same applies when calling stage management and stage staff for scene changes and cues.)

All calls should be made with ladies first and the actors in alphabetical order.

BACKSTAGE CALLS

1   Good evening ladies and gentlemen. This is your half-hour call, half an hour please. Thank you.
2   Ladies and gentlemen the house is now open. Please do not cross the stage. Thank you.
3   Ladies and gentlemen, this is your fifteen-minute call, fifteen minutes please. Thank you.
4   Ladies and gentlemen, this is your five-minute call, five minutes please. Thank you.
5   Ladies and gentlemen, this is your Act One beginners (places) call. Act One beginners (places) please: Miss ..., Miss ..., Mr ... and Mr... (repeat names). Stage management, technical and stage staff stand by please. Thank you.

FRONT OF HOUSE CALLS

The audience must be informed of the fact that the performance will soon be beginning so that they can take their seats in time. The performance must not commence until front of house staff have seated everyone and closed all doors or curtains in the auditorium.

Every venue or theatre has its own method of calling the audience. In some venues the stage management may be responsible for this. Test the call system or bells at every show before the audience arrives.

Here are examples of the kinds of call you will need to make:

1   Good evening ladies and gentlemen, and welcome to the ... theatre. This evening's performance of ...will start in three minutes, three minutes please. Thank you.
(As an alternative, or in addition, you can sound three short bells.)

2   Ladies and gentlemen would you kindly take your seats as this evening's (afternoon's) performance will start in two minutes, two minutes please. Thank you.
(Again you can sound two short bells.)

3   Ladies and gentlemen would you kindly take your seats as the performance will start in one minute, one minute please. Thank you.
(And/or one long bell.)

4   Ladies and gentlemen would you kindly take your seats as the performance is about to start, the performance is about to start. Thank you.
(And/or one long bell.)

Special announcements

In case of fire, accident or understudy appearances an announcement must be made in the auditorium. This may be done over a microphone or by someone in front of the curtain. There should always be someone available, whether it be a member of the stage management or front of house staff, who is reasonably smartly dressed to make such announcements.

① Mac and Polly undress
during song.

② Polly x to USC in B/O
Mac exits DSL.

Scene 3.

③ Mrs. P. enters DSR door
Mr. P. enters DSL door

LX Q19 = B/O
LX Q20 = Sc. Ch. State
S/R QL. = Sc. Ch. GO
S/L
(Clearance from SM.
at end of Sc. Ch.)

F/S 18 = F/S 2
on NARR
D/S/L.
LX 21 = Build
Sc. State.

FS 19 = F/S 2
out.

F/S 20 = Both
F/S on Polly
USC.

ST/BY
LXQS 19-22
F/spot QS 18-21
S/L Q Light
S/R Q Light

26 The Threepenny Opera

MAC: Look at the moon over Soho.
POLLY: I see it, dearest. Feel my heart beating, my beloved.
MAC: I feel it, beloved.
POLLY: Where'er you go I shall be with you.
MAC: And where you stay, there too shall I be.
BOTH:
(1) And though we've no paper to say we're wed
And no altar covered with flowers
And nobody knows for whom your dress was made
And even the ring is not ours –
The platter off which you've been eating your bread
Give it one brief look; fling it far.
For love will *last or else it won't my dear.*
Regardless of where we are. (2)

LXQ19 GO

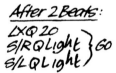

After 2 Beats:
LXQ 20
S/R QLight } GO
S/L QLight

SCENE CHANGE

End of SC.CH.
F/S Q18 GO

3 *Narrator* (3)

To Peachum, conscious of the hardness of the world, the loss of his daughter means utter ruin.

LXQ21 } GO
F/S Q19

Peachum's Outfitting Emporium for Beggars.

To the right Peachum and Mrs Peachum. In the doorway stands Polly in her coat and hat, holding her travelling bag.

MRS PEACHUM: Married? First you rig her fore and aft in dresses and hats and gloves and parasols, and when she's cost as much as a sailing ship, she throws herself in the garbage like a rotten pickle. Are you really married?

F/S Q20 GO

Song lighting: golden glow. The organ is lit up. Three lamps are lowered from above on a pole and the signs say:

RUNNING THE PROMPT CORNER

Always follow a strict routine, for technical and dress rehearsals as well as all performances, to make sure that nothing gets left undone. Your routine should cover the pre-show period, the show itself, and the close-down afterwards.

PRE-SHOW CHECKS

Backstage

Turn on all prompt corner equipment and test head sets, cue lights, monitor, fold-back system, public address system and front of house communication. Then:

■ check the stage: set, furniture, doors, windows
■ check the props
■ check any electrics practicals: lamps, hi-fi, television sets
■ check effects: doorbells, offstage shots
■ check the wings: fire exits clear, set and furniture in their correct offstage positions
■ check that lighting and sound operators have done their checks
■ check all working lights are out, and that there can be a complete blackout on stage.

Front of house

■ make sure the LX preset is up and/or tabs and tab warmers are set
■ inform FOH staff that you are ready and that they can open the house
■ when the house is open make a call backstage to warn people not to cross the stage
Start FOH music according to the director's instruction.

Calls and further checks

1 Call the half hour (35 minutes before curtain up).
2 Check that all actors are in their dressing rooms, and all technical and stage staff have arrived.
3 Call fifteen minutes (20 minutes ahead).
4 Call five minutes (ten minutes ahead).
5 Call beginners (places) and stage staff (five minutes ahead).
6 Make front of house calls and or ring the bells.

7 Check that actors and technicians are in position.
8 After front of house clearance: put all departments and actors on stand-by.
9 Start the performance as per prompt script (noting the time the performance started).

DURING AND AFTER THE SHOW

1 Make the curtain-up announcement backstage.
2 Run the performance using the prompt script.
3 Warn FOH and backstage five minutes before the intermission.
4 Close the first part of the performance as per prompt script (and note the time).
5 Check the intermission change is correct.
6 Call five minutes (ten minutes before the end of the intermission).
7 Call beginners and technical staff (five minutes ahead).
8 Make FOH calls and ring the bells.
9 Check actors and technicians are in position.
10 After FOH clearance: open the second part as per prompt script and run (noting the time again).
11 Warn FOH and backstage five minutes before the end of the performance and call the company for the curtain call.
12 Close the performance and run the curtain call as rehearsed (noting the time again).
13 Give the acting company their next call over the public address system.
14 Wait until the house is clear before walking on to the stage.
15 Turn off all equipment.

THE DRESS REHEARSAL

If time allows, more than one dress rehearsal should be scheduled. The first may show up problems that were missed during the technical rehearsal, and changes may need to be made. A second will give everyone a chance to run the show exactly as it will be on the opening night.
Stage management should run the dress rehearsal exactly as if it were a performance

while being prepared to make last-minute changes. The DSM should time all dress rehearsals as well as performances.

CURTAIN CALLS

Should it not be possible to rehearse the curtain calls before opening night, the director may require stage management to organize them. Write out the director's instructions and put copies in all the dressing rooms.

PHOTO CALLS

Photographs are often taken during a dress rehearsal. The cast should be warned if a photographer is in the auditorium. Alternatively a special photo call may be required. The director will choose which section of

the piece should be photographed. Stage management should see to it that the correct scene is set up on the stage with adequate lighting. A member of stage management should remain on stage to ensure that there is as little delay as possible between scenes.

OPENING NIGHT

The main difference between opening night and dress rehearsal is first night nerves. A great deal of tact and patience may be required to keep the atmosphere backstage calm and well organized.

The other difference is the fact that there is an audience and front of house staff. FOH calls and bells will be needed for the first time, and FOH staff will require the running times of each part of the performance.

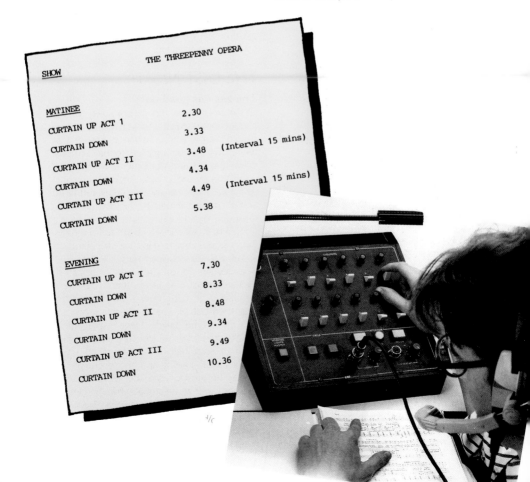

THE THREEPENNY OPERA

SHOW

MATINEE

CURTAIN UP ACT 1   2.30

CURTAIN DOWN   3.33

CURTAIN UP ACT II   3.48   (Interval 15 mins)

CURTAIN DOWN   4.34

CURTAIN UP ACT III   4.49   (Interval 15 mins)

CURTAIN DOWN   5.38

EVENING   7.30

CURTAIN UP ACT I   8.33

CURTAIN DOWN   8.48

CURTAIN UP ACT II   9.34

CURTAIN DOWN   9.49

CURTAIN UP ACT III   10.36

CURTAIN DOWN

DURING THE RUN

Stage manager
(Production stage manager)

The SM is responsible for the setting up of the stage before every performance. You should call the stage management and stage staff early enough for everything to be ready by the half-hour call. Check the set thoroughly before every performance to ensure that everything is in safe working order, and hold yourself responsible for maintenance and repairs.

The SM is also responsible for discipline backstage. So you should ensure that all actors have arrived backstage by the half and that backstage rules are observed.

In addition you should oversee all scene changes and be ready to step in to anyone's job in case of illness. In order to do this you must collect copies of everyone's running plots and cue sheets. These should be kept with the prompt script. Scene change lists and diagrams can be displayed on a wall in the wings for guide/reference during the performance.

Deputy stage manager
(First assistant stage manager)

The DSM should run each performance as per prompt script and follow the list of pre-show checks every time. You should time every performance and write a report on the show. The show report should contain details of anything that went wrong and the reason why. Comments on the size of the audience and how well the performance was received may also be helpful. The director may require a copy of the report and the stage manager should read and sign it before it is copied.

If a prompt is required during the performance give it clearly and loudly enough for the actor to hear. Three or four words is usually enough.

Once the cues have been finalized they can be inked into the script. Use red for standby and green for go. If using a cue light system give each department a different colour.

Assistant stage manager
(Second assistant stage manager)

The ASM should be responsible for setting and maintaining the props.

No changes should be made to set or props without the acting company being informed. Nothing new should be introduced before performance without a rehearsal. Encourage actors to check their own props and set their own quick-change costumes when there are no dressers.

UNDERSTUDIES

The director may not be available to take understudy rehearsals, so it may fall to the stage manager and deputy to organize and oversee them. A prompt script with accurate blocking is essential for understudy rehearsals. Should an understudy be called to appear a rehearsal with the rest of the cast should be held before the performance. If a rehearsal is not possible it is essential that the rest of the company be informed of the change in the cast. The audience should also be informed by putting a slip in the programme or making an announcement before the performance.

THE LAST NIGHT

The get-out (load-out)

Organizing this is the responsibility of the production manager. As with the fit-up you should plan it well in advance. Ensure that there will be enough personnel to take down the set and equipment, and to pack up costumes and props. Arrange transport to return stock to storage places and hired and borrowed articles to their owners. You must also decide which parts of the set are to go into stock and which are to be thrown out. Large rubbish skips can be hired to accommodate the accumulated rubbish.

Because the get-out lacks the anticipatory excitement of the fit-up there can be a temptation to cut corners; but it should be organized just as well. Every safety precaution should be taken. Stage management should strike all props, dressing and furniture from the stage before the set is taken down. All electrical, lighting and sound equipment should be struck from the wings and set. The set can then be struck while the electric department de-rig equipment front of house. Flying pieces, then the floor covering should be struck, followed by the onstage flown lighting equipment.

A.S.M. RUNNING PLOT

SHOW   THE THREEPENNY OPERA

A.S.M.

POSITION   STAGE RIGHT

Before the 1/2   Check and turn on smoke gun U.S.R.

                        Set S.R. props as per setting list.

After the 1/2   Check all personal props as per list.

Act I Places   Check Mr Evans (Macheath) is ready in S.R. wing.

Act I Running Plot

1. End of Prologue   Take umbrella and camera from Mrs Peachum (Miss Shade)
   Approx 7.35 pm   and umbrella from Mr Peachum (Mr McFadden).

2. Sc. Change   On D.S.R. cue light, set the dummies and curtain to
   into Sc. 1   onstage position with crew member B. Enter and exit
   Approx 7.36 pm   through D.S.R. door.

3. Sc. Change   On D.S.R. cue light, strike dummies and curtain to
   into Sc 2   preset position with crew member C. Enter through U.S.R.
   Approx 7.45 pm   door. Exit through D.S.R. door.

PROP SETTING LIST (STAGE RIGHT)   A.S.M.:

SHOW   THE THREEPENNY OPERA   SHEET NO: 1 (of 2)

STAGE RIGHT:

ON PROPS TABLE

PROP	Dress Rehearsal	Perf No.	2	3	4	5	6	7	8
1. Camera (leaded with flash)	✓	✓	✓						
2. 1 green umbrella	✓	✓	✓						
red umbrella	✓	✓	✓						

73

CURTAIN CALLS

SHOW

THE THREEPENNY OPERA

D.S.M.:

END OF ACT III - BLACKOUT - COMPANY EXIT

CALL   LIGHTS UP - B̶...gars/Policemen/Whores enter DSL & DSR Doors

```
    ..          S/L     Mr ...
    ..                  Mr ...
    ...                 Mr ...
                        Miss ...

         Ladies in Centre)
    ) to upper levels S/L and S/R

      ∍nter USL and USR doors

                S/L     Mr ...
                        Mr ...
                        Mr ...

    .. (Jenny) enter DSL door
    . (Lucy)  enter DSR door
      (Brown) enter USC door
      break left
    & Mr ... break right

    Mrs P) enter DSL doors
    ') enter DSR door
       the right

    lly) enter DSL door
    )   enter DSR door

    r) enter USC door
```

ORCHESTRA BOW

DISCRETION

SHOW REPORT

SHOW   THE THREEPENNY OPERA

PERFORMANCE NO.

STAGE MANAGER

THEATRE

DATE

DSM

ACT SC	FOH	UP	DOWN	TIME	Interval/Scene change
ACT I	7.33	7.34	8.37	1.03	17
ACT II	8.53	8.54	9.40	46	16
ACT III	9.55	9.56	10.44	48	

PLAYING TIME 2.37   33

TOTAL RUNNING TIME   3 HRS 10 MINS

ABSENTEES/UNDERSTUDIES: None

House   Full   An excellent response

REMARKS

LX Q 61 and Sound Q 2 were late - DSM cueing error
S/L follow spot's lamp blew in ACT 1 - it was replaced in the interval.
The FOH tabs caught on the pros walls briefly as they came in at the
end of ACT II.

signed by
DSM AND SM

Returns

It is essential that all hired and borrowed articles are returned promptly and in good condition. Keeping the source sheets up to date is very important if everything is to get back to the right place. Valuable sources of free or cheap props can be lost by returning things late or in bad condition.

Scripts

Stage management should collect all the scripts if they are to be returned or kept together as a set.

Prompt script

All lists and paperwork pertaining to the show should be kept with the prompt script and stored as a valuable source of information for future productions.

MUSICALS

Musicals tend to be more complex and on a larger scale than most plays. They require more time to rehearse, both on and off stage, and more time to set up technically. The director, the musical director and the choreographer must all be consulted when working out schedules, and extra time must be found for dance, music and orchestral rehearsals.

REHEARSALS

A larger stage management team is required to organize a musical. For one thing, there may be as many as three sets of rehearsals taking place simultaneously: one for production, one for choreography and one for music. Special consideration must be given to the particular needs of each director when choosing suitable rooms.

The DSM should remain with the director for the production rehearsals, and will most certainly need an ASM to keep all these rehearsals running smoothly. Rehearsal calls will need great care in working out to avoid double booking the acting company. Unless the DSM has had experience of dance notation it is not advisable to try to block dance routines in any detail. But do note where everyone enters and exits and where dancers and chorus move or stand during the non-musical parts of the production.

ORCHESTRA OR BAND

No matter how few musicians there may be, they will need music stands, probably with lights attached, and suitable chairs to sit on. The conductor or musical director will decide where the musicians are to sit, but they will need help to lay out the orchestra pit or space. If the musicians are to sit on stage ensure that they stay within the designated area, away from the acting space. Make a note of how the chairs are laid out and mark the positions in case they have to be moved. When using an orchestra pit it may be necessary to cover it with a lightweight net to prevent articles from rolling or falling from the stage into the pit.

RUNNING A MUSICAL

If you are to cue an opera or dance production it is advisable to be able to read music. This is not essential for musicals, but it does help to have a good ear for music. Make up the prompt script using the text and libretto rather than the musical score. If any cues need to be given during musical passages insert the sheet of music into the script (piano and voice only, not full orchestra). Opera prompt scripts should use the piano and voice score. Write cues as for a play.

The addition of a chorus of singers and dancers to the cast will affect the length of calls during the show. Do not attempt to call them all by name, just call the company for particular musical numbers.

A beginners call for an opera might go: 'Orchestra and beginners please. Ladies and gentlemen this is your act one beginners call. (Call the principals by name – and repeat.) Ladies and gentlemen of the chorus your call please. Ladies and gentlemen of the orchestra to the pit (call the conductor separately). Last call stage management and stage staff.

DANCERS AND SAFETY

It is essential that the stage floor is even, dry and non-slip, and that the stage and wings are well swept. Trays of crushed rosin may be needed in the wings. Some stage surfaces and shoes are inherently slippery so many dancers like to coat the soles of their shoes with rosin to prevent accidents. Alternatively the stage can be sprayed with a solution of water and a sugary liquid such as lemonade.

SINGERS

A dry, dusty atmosphere is not good for singers. The stage area should be sprayed lightly with water before each performance to settle dust and moisten the atmosphere.

CHAPTER 7

EFFECTS

DOOR BANGS, KNOCKS AND KEYS

A door box fitted with a latch or lock and door knocker will give a realistic sound from the wings. The larger the box the louder and deeper the sound.

GLASS CRASH

Use a metal box of broken glass or crockery to make a small crash. Lay a small sheet of glass over the top of the pieces and hit it with a hammer for a sharper sound. Larger crashes are better taped, for safety reasons as well as effect.

DOOR BELL

Fix the door bell or chime on to a wooden base with a battery and door press button. Fix the whole thing on the offstage side of the flat near the appropriate door.

GUNSHOTS

A starting pistol and blanks should be used for a standard pistol shot and a cannon launcher and blanks for a louder report. Always have a spare pistol available and loaded in case of failure. Always keep fire arms and blanks locked safely away. Never leave them lying about. Ear plugs may be needed when firing guns in the wings. Some guns and pistols require a licence. Consult your local police if in doubt.

TELEPHONE

Onstage: run a cord from a practical telephone onstage to a switch offstage which is in turn linked to a suitable mains transformer. (If in doubt ask the electrics department.)

Offstage: if a practical telephone is not available the doorbell apparatus could be used.

Technical rehearsals should be stopped before the following effects are used. They should be demonstrated with everyone standing well clear. If all is well the effect should then be reset and rehearsed into the action of the play.

SNOW

A specially made snow-like substance is available, but in some cases small pieces of white paper are just as effective and much less expensive. A snow bag hanging over the stage from two flying bars should provide an adequate snowfall effect.

RAIN

Dry

Fine sand or rice in a bag similar to the snow bag can be used, provided it is well upstage in front of a backcloth or a cyc.

Wet

A length of flexible pipe with holes pierced in it connected to the mains water supply or water tank in the grid above the flys should provide a shower. Adequate drainage at stage level is essential.

ELECTRICAL EFFECTS

Dry ice and smoke should be dispersed through the correct apparatus. These are electrically operated and usually fall under the auspices of the electrics department. Flash pots and firecrackers should also be electrically operated with instructions being followed meticulously. Again a pyrotechnic licence may be required.

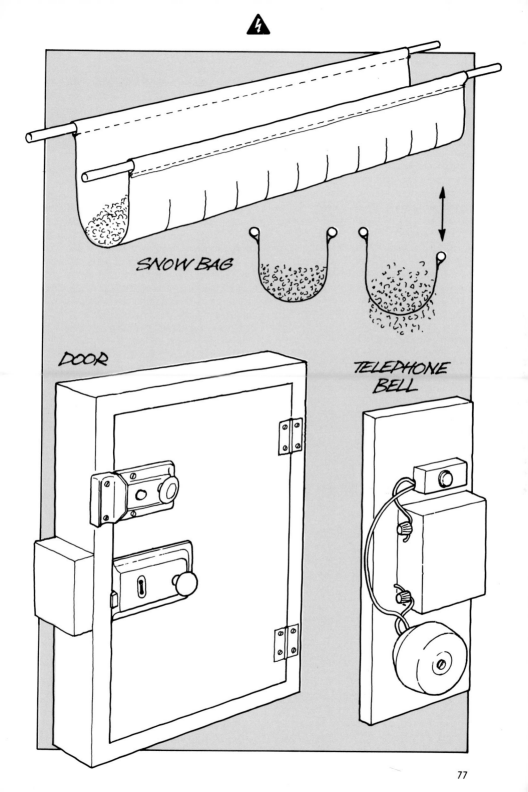

SNOW BAG

DOOR

TELEPHONE BELL

TOURING

Planning venues

No matter how small the production and set may be, or whether the venues are to be proscenium arch theatre, halls or out of doors, it is essential to get as much information as possible before deciding whether or not to use them.

Make out a questionnaire that is relevant to your production. Ideally, someone from the stage management team should visit each venue and ask the questions in person. Otherwise send it through the post. If you are not in a position to refuse a venue that is not quite suitable you will have to be prepared to adapt the production or set, and perhaps even hire equipment if it is not available at the venue. Leave nothing to chance: if in doubt, take it with you.

Transport and packing

Make sure the truck or van you choose is large enough to hold all your set and equipment. Pack the truck carefully to prevent breakages. Collect plenty of blankets and cushions to protect more delicate equipment and ample rope or tough cord to tie flats and pieces of the set to the inside of the vehicle.

Pack dressings and props into skips, crates or strong boxes. Pack boxes so that there is nothing protruding from the top, and tie or tape them down. Use plenty of newspaper for delicate articles. Make packing lists. Each skip or box should bear a list of everything it contains. Find the best way to pack and always do it the same way.

Rehearsals on tour

The company should be called early on the day of the first performance at the new venue. For more complex productions, if there is time, it is advisable to hold a cue-to-cue rehearsal to ensure that the technical aspects are working and plotted properly, and so that the actors get used to the new performance space. If there is not enough time for a rehearsal it is essential to run through all the technical cues and scene changes, especially if new operators and stage staff are to be used.

The actors should also be given the opportunity to explore the new stage and try out the acoustics of the new space.

Scheduling

A technical schedule for a new venue should look something like this:

PRODUCTION SCHEDULE (TOURING)

PRODUCTION MANAGER:

STAGE MANAGER

SHOW:

VENUE:

SATURDAY
0.00 pm
(after performance)

Stage Management strike and pack props, dressings and furniture
Wardrobe pack costumes
SM and crew strike set and load van
LX team de-rig
SM and van travel to next venue

SUNDAY
0.00 am

0.00 pm

Unload van and commence fit up (get in) at new venue
SM team and actors travel to new venue
LX and sound rig and focus

MONDAY
0.00 am

SM team dress the set and set props
SM and crew organize wings
Scene change rehearsal
Wardrobe put costumes in dressing rooms
Lighting

TECHNICAL INFORMATION

COMPANY: SHOW:

VENUE:	Name
	Address
	Phone No
CONTACT :	Management
	Technician /SM

PERFORMANCE SPACE:

Stage or Hall?   Flying-hemp, counterweight
Ground plan?   winch? How many bars?
Dimensions?   Elevation plan?
Height?   Stock - masking, curtains, platforms,
Floor surface?
Obstructions?   Storage space
Wing Space?

ELECTRICS: Equipment in stock - lighting and sound

Lanterns	Amplifiers	Power supply -
Control Board	Tape decks	how many phases sockets -
Effects	Speakers	- 5, 13 and 15 amp
Lighting Positions	Microphones	

COMMUNICATIONS: Public address system
Cue lights
Head sets
Cue desk?

SEATING: Fixed auditorium or chairs?
Platforms or scaffolding?
Capacity?
Who is responsible for fitting it up?

FACILITIES: Dressing Rooms - how many and what size?
Green Room and catering?
Wardrobe space? hanging facilities? washing and drying
facilities? Toilets, wash basins, showers?

ACCESS: Street - any restrictions - parking?
Doors into venue - size?
What floor is performance space/stage on?
Stairs, corridors, corners?
Is there an elevator available? what size?

FIRE REGULATIONS: What are the fire regulations.

RESIDENT STAFF: Stage
Technicians
Wardrobe/Dressers?
Cost?

STAGE FIGHTS AND WEAPONS

Stage fights should be very carefully choreographed and rehearsed. Extra time during the technical rehearsal should be scheduled to rehearse all fights, and actors should be allocated time on stage to run through the fight before every performance.

SAFETY

It is essential to take great care when staging any fight, however brief. Props and settings must be set accurately, as any variation from the way the fight has been rehearsed could cause accidents to the fighters, other actors on stage and even the audience.

Members of the audience should never be seated too close to an acting space where a fight is to take place. Should a sword snap or fly out of an actor's hand it could easily hit one of them.

The stage surface should be even, dry, non-slip and well swept. Lighting should not vary from performance to performance. Weapons should be kept in a good condition.

All swords and firearms must be kept in a locked cupboard and never left unattended during rehearsal or performance. They should only be brought out when required onstage and promptly put back under lock and key afterwards.

BLOCKING

As with dance choreography it is difficult to block a fight without a working knowledge of sword play and unarmed combat. The fight director will document the fight if necessary. Obtain a copy of his notation for the prompt script. Do mark down details of exits and entrances and the movements of the non-fighters onstage.

FIGHT EFFECTS

Blood

To simulate body wounds stage blood is sealed in a plastic bag and strapped under the costume of the fighter. Capsules are available to give the effect of blood coming from the mouth.

Sugar glass

Practically any kind of bottle or glass container is available made from sugar glass. These can be smashed harmlessly against anything — on a fighter's head if required — without any ill effect.

Sticks, staves and clubs

Prop clubs can be made from foam rubber bound with wide tape or gauze. If real sticks and clubs are required, make sure there are no jagged edges, splintery surfaces or cracks, and that they are strong enough to stand up to regular use. Replace damaged weapons promptly.

SWORDS

There are many different styles of foil, rapier and sword available for hire. It is essential to research the correct period and style of weapon. Only use swords especially made for fighting. Dress swords should never be fought with as the blades are not strong enough to withstand heavy use.

Swords should be used in rehearsal as soon as possible. They can vary in weight and the actor will need to use the same sword during rehearsal and performance. New weapons should never be introduced without rehearsal.

Never use a broken or worn sword. Like all weapons they should be well maintained. Clean off rust with oil and steel wool and polish with any metal polish. Blade edges will become pitted and jagged with use and should be regularly filed smooth. Hilts will work loose from the blade and should be tightened regularly with a pair of pliers. Sword belts, scabbards and frogs should fit well and should be kept in good condition.

FIREARMS

As with swords, there are a great many different kinds of pistols, rifles and shotguns available for hire. Research carefully into the period and style. Rehearsal arms should be of the correct weight and size but performance arms need not be introduced until the technical rehearsal.

Guns that are able to be fired on stage are also available, but many will require a special licence. Consult your local police for details. These guns usually use special blanks or a small firecracker as ammunition. Make sure you know exactly what kind to buy by consulting the hire firm when you order the gun. It is essential that guns and ammuntion be locked away safely when not on stage.

Technical rehearsals should be stopped before a gun is fired and a special test made so that everyone knows what to expect when the shot happens. Have a spare gun loaded in the wings in case the gun on stage should fail to fire.

Guns should never be fired close to anyone's head. The report could deafen them. Should the action require someone to be shot at close range it is safer to use a gunshot from the wings. A small maroon will emit some smoke and some flame from the barrel. These create an excellent effect but should always be fired at arm's length and never when near to another person.

Guns that are to be fired must be in good condition and cleaned and oiled regularly. Never use a damaged or cracked fire arm.

To appear to stab someone an actor may have to cheat by turning upstage or by hiding the blade under the arm of the person he is 'stabbing'.

PART TWO
THEATRE ADMINISTRATION

A job description for the administrator of a theatre production will vary according to both the organization and the individual. You might be called the business manager, for example, and be responsible only for the finances of the project. Or you might just look after marketing or publicity and have nothing to do with budgeting or financial control.

You are less likely to take on all three of the major areas described here – financial control, marketing, and house management. But there are distinct advantages in having one person who *co-ordinates* all these functions. That way you can create a coherent team which can partner the production team.

This administrative team works with the production team to achieve the best possible show.

Administrative procedures exist only to support the project and enhance its chances of success. They are not an end in themselves and should never be allowed to thwart the production process.

Different kinds of projects will need different approaches to budgeting and marketing, and different venues. Just like the production team, you should relate to the particular requirements of your project, and like them you should:

■ plan early ■ be specific ■ be flexible.

FINANCIAL CONTROL

What does financial control mean in the context of your group, and why is it important?
It means that you control expenditure and income so financial targets are met and your group remains at least as stable financially after the project as it was before. If finances go out of control and you trust to luck it is inevitable that the production will overspend. It is your job to stop this while at the same time allowing and helping the rest of the production team to achieve their objectives and mount a successful production.

In carrying out your responsibilities and ensuring that budgets are not overspent you should try not to thwart or frustrate the creative members of the production team. If the director and/or the designer want a particular production effect which you know will blow the budget it is very simple to say 'No'. It is harder, more time-consuming, but very important in the interests of the production, to say 'Well, that's going to be very difficult because, as you can see, we don't have that kind of money. But, if you really need this backcloth/antique table/marbled floor, is there another, cheaper way of getting a similar effect? Or is there something else we could cut from the budget?'.

Apparently intractable problems are much more likely to be solved with this kind of co-operative approach in which you regard yourself as an integral part of the production team. Like the other members of the team you will want to play your part in mounting a successful production, and you will not do that if you stand apart from the creative process and frustrate it.

The three stages of financial control set out here are closely related parts of one continous process:

- budgeting
- financial records
- monitoring the budget.

Each stage describes the production in *financial* terms, in the same way as the designs describe the production in visual terms. A designer, for example, will not produce a design which does not suit the particular production envisaged by the director, or which does not suit the particular performance space, and will not design costumes without regard for the actors who have to wear them – or at least, not without risking a major disagreement.

Equally, you must remember that you are administering the finances of a specific production and, like the designer, you must take into account the specific aims, style and constraints of that production, and the financial implications of your venue.

BUDGETING

The process of budgeting and the end result, the budget itself, are equally important.

The process

This helps you and your colleagues to focus on the important features in your production and to anticipate potential problems. Don't pay lip service to early planning. Centre it around the drawing up of an accurate budget. The more work you put in at this stage, the fewer last-minute unanticipated problems there will be. And it is the last-minute problems that cause the frayed nerves and panic expenditure which is very difficult to control. Your aim is to reduce last-minute panic to a minimum.

The budget

By saying what you will spend in each heading you describe the production financially. Be specific. You are describing your production, in your venue. Nevertheless, thoughts about the production will change, and you will have to accommodate these changes in your system.

It is never too early to start drawing up a budget, but it is dangerous to finalize one too early as there is a tendency for it to be inflexible and restrictive.

You will know or you will be given a figure for the net expenditure or net profit on your production. You might be accountable to a committee to which you can return with a request for more funds, but that is unlikely. This figure is the bottom line of your budget sheet and, throughout the process, the target you are aiming at.

Don't expect to hit the target first time. The designer will make several sketches of the set before the final design. So, too, should you make several drafts of the budget to make sure that you are heading in the right direction, and to give you and the production team room for manoeuvre in the critical early stages when thoughts change.

Use the budget sheet format on pages 86-7 for all the stages you go through before you reach the final budget. Date each of them so that in any discussion you can be sure that you are all talking about the same figures. *You will not have all the information you need to complete the budget at each stage. Sometimes you will have to assume things and confirm or change them later. Don't worry about this.* Estimates play an important part in budgeting and you won't know everything that you would like to until the production has finished. For example, in your first attempt at a budget, you may not know where you are going to do the production and, therefore, what venue costs may be involved. This is the very reason for including an estimate of what those costs may be. You should, of course, make it as accurate as possible, but any figure included in a balanced budget will be a yardstick against which to measure more accurate costings as they become apparent.

Income

The income budget is the amount that you are going to keep, and is therefore not necessarily the same as the box office receipts. This will depend on whether you have your own venue or, if not, what kind of deal you have with the venue (see page 110 for the three kinds of agreement). If you do not know your venue when you do your first budget you will have to estimate the kind of seating capacity you are likely to have and the range of prices.

If you intend getting someone else to handle marketing, do so before you are committed to an income budget, and consult closely with them. Do not hand the job over as a *fait accompli*.

However small the venue's seating capacity and however confident you are, do not budget box office income at more than 70 per cent of capacity. Make deductions of tax, royalties, venue's percentage (if any) from that 70 seventy per cent. Bear in mind also that of that 70 per cent a variable proportion will not pay the full rate for a ticket. Your 70 per cent will soon be closer to 50 per cent.

This may seem discouraging, but if you do better, that will be a very welcome windfall. If you do worse the problem will not be as bad as it would have been if you had budgeted at 90 per cent.

Use whatever records you have at your disposal: your own or your venue's box office return from past productions. There will probably be trends which your production will follow unless it is radically different from any previous show.

Catering receipts

If you are doing your own catering, budget carefully for a modest profit. You know how many patrons you expect at each perfomance from the box office budget, how many of these will buy coffee or drinks, and what the profit will be. Don't just make a figure out of thin air. *Calculate* as scientifically as possible.

Grants or sponsorship

If you have a grant or sponsorship absolutely confirmed, include it in your budget. If not, don't.

You may need to draw up a budget to apply for a grant or sponsorship. Present the budget showing a shortfall of the amount you are requesting. Do not automatically boost expenditure figures. Make the budget realistic and honest, or the bodies or companies examining it, who are likely to be more experienced at this than you, will suspect your judgement.

Expenditure

The sample budget sheet gives four main headings of expenditure which are, in broad terms, in order of the degree to which you have control over their level. Administration and venue costs, once you know what the venue is, are going to be much less flexible than production costs.

Administration costs

Records from past productions are particularly valuable in estimating administration costs, as they tend not to vary as much as others. If you do not have records, or if you have reason not to follow them, be as methodical as you can. Consider even apparently small factors such as how much is likely to be spent on photocopying and postage.

A guess is never as reliable as an estimate based on calculation. Don't think that because you are responsible for the budget you have to know all the answers. If you don't, ask someone who does.

If you are not an accountant, or at least extremely knowledgeable about the preparation of accounts, you will need someone who is. Even if you do not need audited accounts at the end of the production, you should aim to have accounts which are as orderly as if they had been audited. So a friendly accountant would be useful; there is bound to be someone associated with your group who would be happy to help or advise you, perhaps for nothing.

Venue costs

If you have your own venue and its costs are borne centrally you need not worry about this heading. In any other case see pages 115-17, especially regarding contras.

Marketing

Before you arrive at a marketing budget there is a planning process you have to go through (see pages 94-101). Before you are able to do that assume as a working figure a marketing budget of 25 per cent of your budgeted box office receipts. This should cover most expenditure under normal circumstances. If you know at a very early stage that you have a particular marketing problem – a new or obscure play for example – increase the budget then.

Production costs

These are, of course, the heart of your budget. Clearly you cannot complete this section without close consultation with the director, designer and stage/production manager. Even then, there will be many unresolved issues. They will explain, however broadly, what their production ideas are. After an initial briefing you can do your first rough budget, making very broad assumptions. At the end of that stage you will have an idea of how good or, more likely, how bad the financial picture is. Take this back to a subsequent meeting. You can explain how you have compiled the budget and the director and designer can say to what extent that reflects their ideas, which may have changed meanwhile. If there is a problem you can share it. Even if you technically have the power to overrule the director and designer it will be counterproductive to invoke that power. They are

BUDGET

PRODUCTION ....

DATE ....

EXPENDITURE   BUDGET   TO DATE

Administration costs
- Stationery
- Photocopying
- Postage
- Insurance
- Telephone
- Bank charges
- Audit fee

Venue costs
- Hire fee
- Display costs
- Publicity contra
- Staff contra

Marketing costs
- Design costs
- Posters
- Leaflets
- Other print
- Newspapers
- Postage
- Merchandising
- Reserve

Production costs
- Fees (Director
-      (Designer
-      (Other
- Set
- Costumes
- Wigs
- Make up
- Props
- Furniture
- Weapons
- Transport
- Lighting/sound
- Musical instruments/scores
- Hire of rehearsal rooms
- Licences/royalties/
-      Scripts

Total expenditure

Budget

EXPENDITURE

INCOME

Box office receipts   . . . .

BUDGET

TO DATE

Less deductions:
   State tax   . . . . . .
   Royalties   . . . . . .
   Others

Net box office receipts

   Catering receipts
   Grants
   Sponsorship
   Other   . . . . .
   Total income   . . . . .
                    . . . . .

Deficit/Profit

more likely to be positive if you are too.

If there is a shortfall you will be asked if you can increase income or reduce another part of the budget. If you have been methodical in devising the rest of the budget you can resist those arguments convincingly. But avoid becoming territorial about the budget, especially in the early stages. The budget and budgeting process are intended to help, not hinder, the production process. As you are working towards the final draft be receptive to ideas that will make it more accurate but, towards the later stages, be firm when you know a suggestion to be unrealistic.

Finally allow a contingency of about 5 per cent of the total budget. This should be enough to cope with relatively small, unexpected problems.

Final working budget

After a few attempts and some consultation you will have devised the final budget for your production. It will be:

■ balanced – that is expenditure and income will be equal, or will differ by an approved amount
■ agreed by the production team. Some might have wished for a higher budget but they have at least been consulted
■ give an accurate description of the show in financial terms.

This budget should now be circulated to the whole production team, clearly labelled as the working budget.

FINANCIAL RECORDS

Accounts are not as difficult as they often look and sound. They are less intimidating if you think clearly about their functions. You will want yours to provide three things:

■ accurate information about the financial state of the production which you will need in order to make important decisions
■ a record of expenditure and income, which you may need for funding bodies, a management committee or your bank
■ information to guide you when compiling any future budgets.

Order forms

If you have a number of different people spending money, or if your budgets are relatively large you should have an order form system. If orders for goods and services are made by only one person there is less need for this.

You do not need to go to a lot of trouble or expense to set up your system: a notebook with numbered pages in triplicate will be sufficient. Each spender should have one. When anything is ordered (goods or services) buyers should write it into their book giving the following details:

■ name and address of supplier
■ value of goods or services

Date	Details		Cheque No.	Total		Sales Tax

- estimated or quoted price
- part of the budget to which the expenditure is allocated
- buyer's signature.

Of the three copies one goes to the supplier, one is kept by the buyer and one goes to the accounts person. If an invoice comes in subsequently which is above the amount estimated on the order form the accounts person will know to question it before payment.

Even when buyers pay for something on the spot, it helps if they write out an order form, if only to have it on record. The receipt should go straight to the accounts person along with the 'confirmation' order form. In this way both parties have the same record of purchases and commitments.

If used properly, order forms give a complete picture of spending committed to date.

Ledger

This is a record of payments made or agreed. It is a grid sheet containing vertical columns corresponding to your budget headings, and horizontal lines for entries, in date order, of payments. It needs to be wide enough to accommodate all your headings comfortably. You can combine headings to save space, but only do so if there are likely to be a few entries which are easy to identify.

When an invoice comes in, match it with its order and compare them. If they disagree ask the buyer why that is so. When you have resolved that, or if there is no discrepancy:

- write 'approved' on the invoice, sign it and indicate the budget heading to which it is allocated
- write and dispatch a cheque
- enter the date and cheque number in the left-hand columns of your ledger sheet. Enter the amount paid in the 'total' column and in the column for the appropriate budget heading. (Occasionally you will divide one payment between two or more different headings.)
- if the amount paid includes VAT (sales tax) and you can reclaim it, enter the amount in the VAT column and put the net amount in the other column(s). If you cannot reclaim the tax just enter the whole amount
- file the paid invoices in alphabetical order of suppliers.

By drawing a line and adding up each column you can find out exactly how much has been spent to date in each heading. If you add this to the 'committed' amounts on order forms you will know what your total commitment figure is in each column. When monitoring your expenditure and income you can cross-check this financial information with that provided by the spenders.

Cash flow planning

This means ensuring that you have enough cash at any one time to pay your bills when you have to. You may have budgeted, quite correctly, that your production will make a profit. If you don't work out your cash flow you may not realize that expenditure occurs a long time before income. You may have to pay for the venue in advance, or pay cash for materials. But there may not be any income until the very late stages of booking; or if it consists in part of a grant, some of this

...ney	Photocopies	Postage	Insurance	Telephone	Bank Charges	Audit Fee		

may not be paid until you submit final accounts, after the production.

Your particular cash flow requirements will depend on your circumstlances. If your project is funded by a group with resources, this may cushion your cash flow. But if that is not so you must plan it for yourself. Prepare a cash flow chart covering each week of the production period, from the time spending or booking starts, whichever comes first.

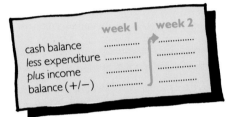

This will alert you in advance to a potential cash flow problem which you can solve either by delaying expenditure or advancing income. If you have to delay paying bills tell your creditors why. They will almost certainly understand and be grateful that you have taken it seriously. You can also ask for an advance of grant income or sponsorship, if you have any. If you are an independent group with its own bank account talk about cash flow to your bank manager very early.

MONITORING THE BUDGET

Even if you have exercised the greatest possible care in devising your budget actual expenditure will not always follow it exactly. You will need a way of:

■ reducing possible variations between estimated and actual expenditure
■ knowing what variations there are when they happen and calculating what effect they have overall
■ taking steps to put finances back on the right track if necessary.

Reducing variations

Uncertainty about the size and nature of the budget is a common cause of overspending. Having consulted about it and circulated copies you must also make sure that indi-

viduals know for which parts they are responsible. In subsequent production meetings, when detailed discussions about parts of the production are held, they will then know exactly how much money they have to provide what is being asked of them. When you give out the working budget you could annotate each heading with the initials of the person responsible for it, or you could also give each one their own set of figures extracted from the main budget.

Ask each spender in the production team (or the production manager) to give you a further breakdown of the production budget showing in detail how it will be allocated. This exercise will encourage them to think about their budgeting constraints and anticipate and deal with any problems early on.

Effect of variations

Variations will still happen, and you must know about them. Use a budget update form (see pages 86-7), which is in the same format as the budget sheet with an extra column.

From the time that working and spending begin in earnest – rarely later than a month before the first performance – complete the form every week. Fill in the budget figures in each heading, which will not change now. You will have some information about spending from your order form or other records, but you must supplement it. Ask the spender/production manager to provide you with a weekly note of what they have spent so far, and what they expect to spend in the future (the committed expenditure). Check the figure against your own records. Encourage them to be completely realistic. It does not help anyone to store up financial problems until the last moment. Underspending is as important as overspending, but not many will report that.

Go through the same process with income. You may not get a clear idea of the way booking is going until very late, and in any case you may take the view that slow business will pick up. But there may be significant factors that cause you to revise the targets up or down.

Fill in the actual figure so far, plus the anticipated ones in each heading, and complete the form, apart from the contingency. You will see immediately what the net effect is at the bottom of the form. Circulate copies of the form to the production team so that everyone can see how the production finances are progressing and how their spending co-ordinates with others.

Actions

If the budget update reveals an anticipated surplus: increase the contingency sum to include it.

If it reveals an anticipated shortfall:

■ discuss with the production team money-saving changes to the production
■ if all else fails reduce or eliminate your contingency so that the budget is still balanced.

Using the contingency is obviously easiest, but dangerous in the early stages: once gone it is gone forever. If there is another crisis later on you will have to ask for production savings at a time when they are much more difficult to make.

It should be made absolutely clear that only the person finally responsible for the budget and its control may use the contingency. Do not let other people think that they can stretch their own budgets because the contingency will save them. If they all think this you will soon be in serious financial trouble! One person must have an overview of expenditure and income.

As when devising the original budget approach the question of production savings in as positive a way as possible. You are then more likely to get a positive response from the production team. Do not take the attitude that they are being irresponsible, thoughtless and foolish. It is much more likely that they are simply trying to make your resources stretch as far as possible, and have miscalculated. If this is so you should *help* them to solve the problem.

Final accounts

If you keep the records described here you will have accounts in such good order that with very little tidying up they can become *final accounts* which can be audited very quickly if that is necessary. You will have to judge the right time to close the accounts: not so soon after the production that some items of expenditure are unresolved; not so late that your committee is kept waiting.

Your ledger sheet will provide you with final *expenditure* figures. Use the same headings from the earliest budget onwards so that there is consistency throughout your financial control system. Then present the final accounts in a form as close as possible to the other documents: with the same headings, in the same order.

It is particularly helpful to present final accounts on one sheet of paper, so you may have to consolidate several subheadings (for example, stationery, photocopying, and postage or costumes, wigs, and make-up). Put final income figures on the same sheet, above expenditure if you make a profit, below expenditure if you make a loss.

MARKETING

PLANNING YOUR CAMPAIGN

Whatever your project and however large or small your venue you are more likely to achieve the income you need if you plan your campaign carefully, specifically and well in advance. You will then be more likely not only to balance your books but also to provide the production with the audience it needs to be a success.

As in every other aspect of mounting a production, forward planning is supremely important. It is also crucial in marketing to remain constantly in touch with the the product. If you don't know the product well you will not sell it effectively. Your marketing strategy will need to be mapped out weeks or months in advance, but be alert to the likelihood of having to adapt it to new conditions. The production may well change in rehearsal or throw up a useful selling angle. Equally some features of your strategy might not be bearing fruit and will need to be changed.

It is quite likely that you will not have as much time as you would like. Do not be intimidated if some of the timescales suggested here are impossible for you. Adapt them to your own needs. You must make maximum use of all your resources, especially your time, and a few days spent planning will pay dividends later. Before you rush into print with a poster or leaflet prepare your campaign in the following areas.

READ THE PLAY

Even if you think you know it very well, read the play again. You will be surprised how your perception of it will change when considering it in the context of planning a marketing campaign.

WORK OUT DEADLINES

Your campaign will centre on a series of deadlines which will probably be dictated by other people and other organizations, and will therefore be largely outside your control. Find out what the deadlines are, even if you are not sure in the earliest stages that they will necessarily concern you. It is impossible to generalize about deadlines because they will depend on specific local factors, but if you check the following you will be covered:

■ the date by which you should provide copy and a graphic image (see page 102) for your venue's marketing/subscription list and/or seasonal brochure if appropriate.

■ if the venue itself does not contact schools and other potential group bookings, determine the date by which you will write to them yourself. This is a waste of time, money and energy two weeks before the event: two months is an ideal lead-in time to allow teachers, for example, to make all their arrangements

■ work your print deadline back from the

date on which it is needed – this might be stipulated in your contract with the venue, especially if you are sharing box office receipts. Assume that you will need the print two months before the opening night, and allow another month before that for design, printing and distribution.

IDENTIFY SELLING POINTS

At the earliest opportunity, certainly before you think about poster design or copy, list the reasons why anyone should buy a ticket for your production. This is best done in a brainstorming session with colleagues, ideally including the director. Do not question or analyse them as they arise: let ideas flow uninhibitedly. Write everything down, however trivial or absurd it seems, and you should have a list of twenty or so ideas. Now analyse them. Duplications will be important because they will show what might be the core of the production's attraction, and apparently trivial ideas may become useful when considered and refined.

After analysis you should have a list of perhaps fifteen strong selling points (abbreviated as SSPs). Concentrate on the theatrical experience you are offering: you are not listing the paragraph headings for an examination answer.

The SSPs will inform the selling from now on, but can of course be up-dated if important new ideas emerge during preparation or rehearsals. In particular be on the alert for ideas, phrases or images which could be useful later. The SSPs will form the basis of what you say in copy and graphic images, and if you get stuck you should always return to them.

You will almost certainly not have access to the kind of sophisticated marketing research information available to industry, so that in drawing up your list you will not be able to avoid making assumptions about the market and what is likely to appeal to it. Your local theatre may have undertaken some kind of market research in the past and it will be useful to you now if you can get hold of it. You are probably a regular, enthusiastic and knowledgeable theatre-goer, but do you know how a more typical member of the general public decides what to see? Do your own research. You may not have time to make it detailed or extensive. But ask friends how they find out about what is going on in the arts, and what makes them decide to buy tickets, or, more likely, not to. Most important of all, if they are favourably disposed, ask what particular factors might move them to buy your tickets?

In many cases it is not the play itself that will attract or repel them. It is often something depressingly mundane such as the accessibility of the theatre, car-parking or late-night transport. Your research should give you a few more SSPs to add to the list.

DRAWING UP MATRICES

This is a technique which matches your selling points to potential audiences, and describe how you can sell tickets to them. The illustrations are only examples. You will have your own SSPs and your own potential audience, both of which will depend on all your circumstances. Drawing up your own matrices will focus your attention on what is possible for you. In some ways the process is more important than the finished product.

Matrix A

Here, list your SSPs in the left-hand column and the potential audience (the 'market') across the top. Simply put a a cross in the intersecting box if the SSP is of particular relevance to a section of the market. As you are doing it you will sometimes think that you are unncessarily complicating something that is basic common sense. Most of it is, but you are organizing that common sense in a way that will pay dividends when you are undertaking the actual marketing activities.

Matrix B

Now match the marketing activities to the markets that you have already identified in Matrix A – in other words, how you are going to tell those people why they should buy tickets. Your marketing activities can be anything you can think of, but the example gives the most obvious.

You might find it helpful to circle some of your crosses if you think something is particularly important, or put in a question mark if you are not sure. You will also find that the matrices take shape more quickly and usefully if several of you do them together.

MATRIX A

	EXISTING AUDIENCE: SUBSCRIBERS	CLUB/ ORGANIZA-TION	SCHOOLS	STUDENTS	LOCAL THEATRE-GOERS	LOCAL 'NEW' AUDIENCE	THEATRE-GOERS FROM A DISTANCE	SPECIAL INTEREST GROUPS
COMPANY/SOCIETY'S REPUTATION	×	×		×	×		⊗	
ENJOYABLE NIGHT OUT - AMUSING	×	⊗		×	×	⊗		
SET TEXT IN PERFORMANCE			⊗	×				
SPECIAL WORK WITH SCHOOLS			⊗					
LOW PRICES/ CONCESSIONS	⊗	×	⊗	⊗				
ACCESSIBLE VENUE: PARKING, ETC.								
'NEW' EXPERIENCE - PERSONAL DEVELOPEMENT						×	×	
LOCAL INTEREST		×						
POPULAR MUSICAL		×	× ?		⊗			
RELEVANCE TO SPECIAL ISSUE		×		× ?		×		
SPECIAL EVENT - NEW PLAY	⊗			×				×
LIVE PEFORMANCE - NOT TV OR FILM			×	×		×	×	×
EASY TO BOOK						⊗	×	

MATRIX B

	EXISTING AUDIENCE: SUBSCRIBERS	CLUB/ ORGANIZA-TION	SCHOOLS	STUDENTS	LOCAL THEATRE-GOERS	LOCAL 'NEW' AUDIENCE	THEATRE-GOERS FROM A DISTANCE (Groups / Individ.)		SPECIAL INTEREST GROUPS
LEAFLET									
POSTER		×	×	×	×				
DISPLAY ADS			×	×	×	×	×	×	×
LETTER					×	×			
PHONE SALES		×	×		×	×		×	
DISPLAY FOH		×	×				×		×
OTHER DISPLAY					×		×		×
PRICE INCENTIVE									
TRAVEL PACKAGE		×	×						
PERSONAL CONTACT			×	×	×				
MEDIA CONTACT	×	× (?)	×		×	×			×

95

TARGETS AND TICKET PRICING

The budget will have told you what your income target is. If you have not drawn up the budget yourself make sure that you know very clearly what your target is. Do not settle for being told that you should do as well as possible. You need to know both what you are aiming at and what your budget is for achieving the target. You must have a way of measuring your own performance.

Your income target will not necessarily be the same as your box office target. The latter will almost certainly be higher and you must calculate what it has to be in order to generate the right income. From the box office income you may have to deduct sales tax and a royalty for the author if the play is in copyright. Your contract with the management of your venue may give them a percentage of the box office receipts. All this means you could well 'lose' half of the receipts, so it is particularly important to know what the deductions are and therefore have a very clear idea of what gross box office income (before deductions) will give you the correct net income (after deductions). If you have not been told what the contractual arrangement is with the venue make a point of asking so that you know of any factors that will affect your income.

When you know your box office target you can start to calculate ticket prices, if this is appropriate. It is possible of course that you are in a venue – an established theatre for example – with its own price structure from which it never departs. Even if this is the case you should give some thought to the system of concessionary prices and schemes, which could still be varied. If you have control over your prices you should spend some time getting it right.

As you analyse your matrices (see previous page) you will have to have worked out your base prices and concession rates, but do not be afraid to return to them if you have second thoughts. Nothing is fixed until you go into print.

Ticket pricing

When calculating ticket prices use all the information at your disposal. If you can get them, look at box office records or returns for similar productions in the past. Try not to rely on memories, however recent, of how well shows have done in the past. 'Quite good' is meaninglessly subjective and in any case doesn't translate into a statistic. Unless you are doing something completely novel (in a new and unusual venue, for example) a pattern should emerge and you should be able to estimate, at least in approximate terms, the realistic likely attendance.

In approximate terms the estimated gross box office receipts (see above) divided by the likely attendance will give you an average ticket price. But as you will give concessions to some groups of ticket buyers the full ticket price will have to be higher than the average. If you have records of other productions you can check what proportion of ticket sales have been at full price and what at the concessionary rates. If not assume that half your tickets will be sold at some kind of concessionary rate.

If the prices you are working around at this stage are significantly higher than is normally paid for your kind of show locally there is clearly something wrong. Most likely the original income target is too high. You might, with hard work and careful planning, increase attendances by 10 per cent over the average of past prodcutions. A 20 per cent increase would be very high. More than that would be unlikely. If your target is wrong you will stand helplessly by, counting the shortfall on each performance – a shortfall that can never be recouped.

Never forget that every unsold ticket is a dead loss, even less saleable than yesterday's newspaper. A concessionary structure should:

■ sell tickets that would otherwise remain unsold

■ indicate the sections of the community you are trying to attract.

There is no limit to the number of concessionary schemes you could devise. But while considering them, think ahead to the difficulties of explaining them simply in print. Schemes that are too complex can be counter-productive, especially if you are aiming at relatively inexperienced theatre-goers. If they can't grasp the details easily they will give up and fail to buy.

As always, be specific. Think of your particular marketing needs when devising your concessions. Are there particular groups you would like to attract? Are there particular performances that will be difficult to sell? Here are some ideas:

■ if the first performance is hard to sell, which might be the case with a new play, offer a special price for the first night. Two tickets for the price of one, or four for two, is good because it doubles the audience. This is especially useful if the press are coming that night as a good house helps the actors and should help inspire favourable reviews

■ offer unsold tickets very cheaply, say half an hour before the performance on a stand-by basis for the general public or for identifiable groups

■ offer a family ticket – reduced price for two adults and two children. It really doesn't matter whether they are strictly all part of the same family

■ have special rates for identifiable groups: children, students, senior citizens, unwaged.

These concessions will to some extent fulfil any social obligations that you might feel. But think carefully about what concessions are appropriate to your production. They are also a way of targeting sales. When you send a leaflet or a letter to schools, don't just tell them that the show is on, but make them a special offer, telling them that you want their business so much that you are giving them a special rate.

ANALYSING MATRIX A

Your finished matrices show your campaign in outline, and whatever changes arise, it will not change fundamentally.

The matrices describe your campaign and how you are going to sell the number of tickets you have already calculated to be necessary to achieve your box office target. This must all be done within your budget, and is less difficult than it sounds. Matrix A describes the audience you are aiming at, so:

■ estimate how many people in each target group (along the top of the matrix) will buy tickets. Be realistic. Use any past records to help get an accurate figure. Be cautious
■ calculate how close these figures take you to your target
■ if you are under target re-examine how you could best increase sales.

In many cases you will be making educated guesses. But you should be fairly certain of how many subscribers among your or the venue's regular audience will come. If they are subscribers there is less of a problem.

If your play is a text set for examination you can rely on a significant audience from schools. Even if it isn't there may be a close connection with a play that is set. It may be by the same author, or be from the same period, or on the same subject. If there is such a connection encourage schools and colleges to bring students.

If there is a special-interest group you may get some kind of audience from it, but don't overestimate it. Specialist groups can be a useful way of picking up a few extra sales, but unless they are specifically theatre-going groups, they are no more likely to go to the theatre than anyone else. In identifying them as a group you are simply able to target them as people who have one extra reason for coming to your show.

Other target groups are even less reliable and therefore more difficult to estimate. 'Theatre-goers' who are not subscribers, wherever they live, are the people who, when asked, exaggerate how often they attend theatre. They say 'quite often' when they really mean two or three times a year. They see themselves as theatre-goers, so

they are likely to respond to publicity, but they are still difficult to target and pin down. They will respond to publicity material if they see it, or see it often enough, and will make up their minds very late.

New audiences are practically impossible to quantify. They may overlap with and be contained within other groups. Some students will be coming to the theatre for the first time, as will some individuals in the special-interest groups. But unless you have very good reasons to do so you should not count on significant numbers in this group. There are, very occasionally, spectacular exceptions. A new show about a local subject will sometimes create massive interest in the area and non-theatre goers will flock in. When they do they often create more excited and exciting audiences than usual. But for the most part you must assume very small numbers of newcomers.

Target shortfall
When you have worked out your target numbers you may have a shortfall. If you have to increase sales you will find it easiest to do so among the regular theatre-goers, subscribers, schools and colleges. It becomes increasingly difficult as you get to the less committed groups.

You should avoid increasing ticket prices if you have had a shortfall. In your preparation, you have assessed how much you can charge: if you now increase that without very good reason you will encounter price resistance and have an even greater shortfall.

When you have finished this part of the exercise you should know where your audience is coming from, how much they will be paying, and to which groups you are going to pay extra attention.

ANALYSING MATRIX B

This outlines the campaign that will sell the tickets to the groups identified in matrix A. Again, you will need to assess the matrix and, in particular, cost the marketing activities described in the left-hand column. Looking at the two matrices together it will be clear which things are going to be central to your campaign. Again, they are likely to be the obvious things: but identifying them clearly will help you to organize your campaign in the most effective way.

In drawing up and budgeting your priorities for each selling activity you will be balancing three factors:

■ selling power: how many tickets is it likely to sell?
■ cost: can it be achieved within the budget?
■ long-term effect: does it convey a general message about your group?

This is where you should take a little time to consider the most effective ways of using your limited resources.

You might be tempted to start designing a poster before you do anything else. A poster will almost certainly feature in the campaign, but look at the matrices. A leaflet is going to be far more important in getting to the core audience. This is fairly common. A poster is important because it is an easy way of publicizing widely that a show is on and conveying some kind of graphic image. But a leaflet, which people can choose to pick up, take away, read and reread at leisure, is more likely to *sell tickets*.

You may even find that ideally you would like more than one leaflet – perhaps one for the general public and one for students; you will, after all, be telling them quite different things. But you will not be able to afford all that you would like. You will have to make priorities, cost all the marketing activities and decide which you need most. Leave yourself a contingency of 10 per cent of the publicity budget to cover unforeseen costs.

Image building

Judging what the best marketing activities are is not always easy. The fact that you will probably have a small budget makes it all the more important to spend wisely. But your task will be further complicated by pressure to do more than just sell tickets. The group you belong to will also want to convey something about itself. This message may be very broad: "This group is amateur but has professional standards", or fairly specific: "This group is young and aims principally at a young audience" or "We are a well-established group presenting popular plays in a fairly conventional way".

This 'positioning' process – building a public image and your consequent appeal to particular audiences – often happens by accident. But every decision your group makes will affect it: the plays you do, how you design and present them, where you do them and, most important of all from a marketing point of view, how and to whom you sell them.

Positioning will affect the emphasis you choose to place on different marketing activities. There may be a new and specific problem you have to address. Perhaps you are doing the kind of play not normally associated with your group. Perhaps the last play you did (or even the last two or three) were unsuccessful.

If, for example, you see a need to re-establish yourself after a few years' decline you might decide to have higher-quality posters, bigger leaflets, more colours, a larger print run of each, or more newspaper advertisements than usual. You must decide what you need, and take account of increased expenditure if there is any.

If you are starting a new group it is particularly important to think carefully about the image you want to establish. All the decisions about the various target groups and marketing activities are more significant because, if you are successful, you will be creating a pattern for the future. So take time with your colleagues to think about your aims. Why have you formed your group? What kind of audience do you want to serve? What kind of plays will you do and in what ways?

A graphic designer, if you are lucky enough to be able to afford one or have a friendly one who will help you, will be able to translate your aims into graphic terms. You will then have a logo – the name of your group in a particular typeface, with or without a symbol – that will always be associated with you. You will also have a house-style for print – a particular way of designing posters and leaflets – which, used with the logo, will be associated with you. You may think this will restrict the variety of design possibilities, but it does not.

EXECUTING YOUR CAMPAIGN

During your preparation you will have been getting a clearer idea of the shape of your campaign. You will know your deadlines, and at that time you will have to commit yourself to specific activities. *But still be prepared to be flexible.*

Although you will achieve better results by planning, marketing is not an exact science, and you will undo all your good work if you are not responsive to outside events. Above all, remain in touch with the production you are selling. It can and will change. Be aware of that and be prepared to adapt your approach if necessary.

If at any time you lose track of specific parts of your campaign return to your matrices. Match each activity in matrix B to the target audience, however broad that might sometimes be. You are undertaking each activity for a reason, and the way you execute it should relate to that reason.

At the centre of your campaign will be three things:

■ printed material of all kinds to be designed and distributed
■ press advertising; press reports, features and reviews
■ a box office operation or more likely, several box office operations.

PRINT

There are three principle kinds of printed material, some or all of which will feature in your campaign:

■ posters of various sizes
■ leaflets or brochures
■ letters to individuals or organizations.

Each has its own function. Posters advertise your show in a very broad way in that, even if they are displayed in relatively private places, they can be seen by anyone who passes. Leaflets are more likely to be distributed in places where potential theatregoers will see them, and they are much more likely to pick one up. Letters are the most specific of our three main printed marketing activities, in that you will write them for and send them to individuals and groups to tell them things which would not be relevant to the general public.

Some features will be common to all three kinds of print. Indeed, it is a distinct advantage to have design echoes throughout your campaign so that all the material you produce combines to have a cumulative as well as an individual effect. But, in other respects, particularly the copy you use on the print, you should take who the recipient is into account.

For each kind of print: posters, leaflets and letters, you must cover three equally important areas:

■ distribution and display
■ design and layout
■ copywriting.

It is a common mistake to spend more time on design than on distribution or copywriting. Pay equal attention to all three. They are mutually dependent. A beautifully designed poster or a skilfully worded leaflet are wasted if nobody sees them.

DISTRIBUTION AND DISPLAY

Look at distribution and display before committing yourself to a design. You must discover *how much* print you can use effectively, and what sizes and shapes are going to be possible. The quantity will affect the price and therefore, to some extent, the how sophisticated the design is. The sizes and shapes will certainly affect your design flexibility and perhaps the amount of copy you can use. You will also, of course, not want to waste money buying more print than you can use.

You may be playing a theatre with its own distribution system. This is fine, but it will probably only cover well-established and relatively conventional outlets.

You may want to supplement this with your own distribution system. First, explore all free systems of both distribution and display. Local authorities will often allow you free use of systems by which they distribute material to schools and libraries – and don't forget your neighbouring areas if it is important on your matrix to reach, say, theatre-goers from a distance. One quick telephone call should tell you whether this is possible, where the pick-up point is, and how many leaflets or other material to provide.

You may know of other free methods of distribution. If not, consider paid-for distribution, which is often surprisingly cheap and can be extremely effective. Leaflets can sometimes be slipped into local newspapers for a very small charge. The mail delivery service may operate local schemes where, again for a small charge, leaflets can be delivered to addresses within a specified area. The great merit of such schemes (there may be more in your area) is that, because you are paying for them, you can choose which areas your material is going into and therefore target it very carefully to those which you think will provide your audience. Discuss these ideas with the postal services and they will tell you about various bulk mailing schemes. Their expertise will be very useful because you are engaging in direct mail, which is a very specialized subject.

Look for free display sites for posters in the usual places – shops, libraries, (probably in the same distribution system as for leaflets) and public notice boards. Before you think about design or print, make sure you know what size posters are acceptable in the display sites. If few sites will take large posters it may not be worth your while to print any, or you could print just a few for selected sites. This is a particularly important financial consideration. The cost of each poster (the unit cost) gets proportionally much higher as the size increases, so you should certainly avoid over-ordering them. The theatre you are using may have its own paid-for poster sites which you will doubtless have to pay for directly or indirectly, but you should look carefully at their cost before considering them seriously for yourself.

DESIGN

The design of posters and leaflets (graphic design) is as important as that of sets and costumes. It is also a different and distinct skill. Good set or costume designers will not necessarily be good graphic designers although they may be a useful source of good visual ideas. As the person responsible for producing print as part of a co-ordinated marketing campaign, you may be designing the poster yourself or you may be working with someone else. Either way, there are basic guidelines to follow to maximize your impact.

Brief your graphic designer clearly after he or she has read the play – make sure they do read it. If you are the graphic designer go through this process with someone else, perhaps the director, as the briefer. Discuss the particular angle the production will take, and your list of strong selling points. Remember the golden rule that you are designing print for a specific production. Graphic designers are as likely to resort to standard formulae as anyone else and you should stop this. Every aspect of the graphic design will convey a message about your production. If your graphic designer indicates gothic lettering on a poster for a Shakespearian tragedy, for example, be aware that some people who see it will think that your production will have wrinkled tights and costumes made of old curtains. This may not be what you want a potential audience to think!

As part of this briefing process, as well as establishing the desired overall image tell the graphic designer clearly:

- what quantity of print you need
- what your budget is
- what your timescale is
- how much room has to be found for informative copy.

The graphic designer will be able to tailor the design to your budget, particularly with regard to the number of colours you can have. Equally, the graphic designer will be able to tell you how you can economize and achieve apparently expensive effects at minimum cost. You can, for example, get an apparently four-colour poster by mixing two colours on coloured paper. You can achieve another dramatic effect with a colour merge, where a dark colour starts at the top of the poster, lightening to white in the centre and then darkening to the second colour towards the bottom. *Good print — that is well-designed print — need not cost more than bad print.* Although your graphic designer will doubtless come up with ideas, you can learn much by paying a visit to a friendly printer.

A graphic designer or a printer will explain to you what shapes and sizes of print are available. The decision about what sizes of poster to print should depend on what display outlets you have. Equally, the decision about sizes and shapes of leaflet should be based on the uses to which you are putting them. You may be tempted to be unusual, and have a different size or shape of leaflet. But there are standard shapes for a reason — racks in theatre foyers and information centres tend to take standard sizes. If a mailing list, either your own or perhaps that of your venue, is a central part of your campaign do not print a leaflet that does not fit a standard-size envelope. Think through the consequences of your decisions.

When you have briefed the graphic designer, ask for an explanation of the general idea in very broad terms so that you can check that you are on the same wavelength. It will be difficult and expensive to alter later, and you will have wasted valuable time.

The graphic designer or whoever is designing the poster will go away and work on the ideas and produce a graphic image and a typeface for the print.

THE GRAPHIC IMAGE

The graphic image is an illustration (photograph or drawing) which is reproduced on your poster and which summarizes the production or important elements of it. You may be able to provide this for the graphic designer — it might be a photograph or a painting which has been a key source material for the director and set/costume designer. If this is so be careful of several things:

■ make sure you can get the rights to reproduce it. A photograph in a book will credit the photographer, and you should get permission to reproduce it from the publisher or the photographer

■ a photograph or painting will lose some of its impact when combined with typographical information. It might tend to be too busy and distract from, rather than help to focus on, important points

■ a full-colour image might not be so effective when translated into the one or two colours and half-tones that are available to you. Sometimes the simplification involved in adapting an image for a two-colour poster makes it clearer. Think it through and experiment with a photocopier and coloured pens — highlighting pens and liquid paper are very good for this

■ be aware that when it appears on a poster, however amended or simplified, an image may have a different effect from that intended. A photograph of an ancient Greek vase showing a young girl fighting a bull may seem like a perfect graphic image for *Antigone*. But there is a danger of it looking like a poster for an exhibition of Greek pottery rather than a piece of theatre. There are similar dangers with reproductions of classical or contemporary paintings.

There are two solutions to these problems. One is to 'treat' the image — that is to put it through a photographic process that in some way distorts it so that it looks more theatrical. Obliterate some details to make room for information, and at the same time concentrate on the parts that convey the message you really want. A graphic designer or printer can tell you what processes are available to do this.

The other solution, of course, is to create your own image. You could set up your own photographic session with the actors, but at the very early stage at which it would be needed you are unlikely to have the costumes. You could use head shots, but it may be that you do not even have the actual actors at this stage. Another possibility is full shots with mock-ups of the costumes, but the latter runs the risk of not relating closely enough to the actual production costumes. So an original piece of artwork is an attractive option because you can tailor it exactly to your requirements. The graphic designer or a friendly artist could do this.

THE TYPEFACE

The typeface is the specific style of lettering for the title, which you should use whenever possible when mentioning the play. It is easiest to pick a standard typeface that most printers stock so that if you place press advertisements, for example, you can ask for the title to be printed in that typeface.

It is a good idea to ask your printer to produce a number of 'bromides' of the title in varying sizes. These are printing-quality black and white copies with very high contrast, which you can give to a printer who doese not stock that typeface or which you can use very successfully on a photocopier.

On a poster or leaflet the graphic image and title will be seen together. It is very effective, but requires rather more sophisticated design skills, to go one stage further and integrate image and title into one piece of artwork. On the whole you would only do this if you have a substantial budget for producing a number of bromides of that artwork – the kind of budget that you are not likely to have without a fairly long run and a large seating capacity.

The essential point behind the image and the title typeface, whether they are integrated or not, is that you should use them as often as possible whenever the play is mentioned. The public will then see the image repeatedly and will identify it as that of your production. By repeating the same image you will be compounding its effect and so maximizing the impact derived from a limited budget.

Similarly, on all print, keep your company's name in its own typeface (you can get bromides of it in the same way) so that a kind of brand image develops.

LETTERS AND CIRCULARS

The importance of repeating the chosen image applies not only to the most obvious kinds of print (posters, leaflets and brochures), but also to letters and circulars. You will doubtless be sending some letters to potential group bookers. The impact will be greater if you spend a little time and money on design. In this case you can almost certainly do your own designing, whether or not you consider yourself a graphic designer.

The cheapest way of doing a circular letter is to reproduce it on a duplicator, but the results are often of poor quality, the kind of quality that suggests the adjective amateur in its worst sense. You will get a very much better quality if you use one of the local 'instant print' shops. It will cost a bit more, but bear in mind that the true cost of producing apparently cheaper but poorer-quality print is very much higher if it does not produce the intended sales.

When designing your letter, experiment with blocks of type – perhaps different kinds and sizes if you have access to a golf ball typewriter or word processor – the bromides of the title and, if you have them, the graphic images. When you have devised a layout you like, take it to a printer and he can print immediately, on coloured paper if required. You must take the decision as to whether in your case this kind of expenditure is worthwhile. If you are sending out only a limited number of letters (say to the press), it is probably more economical to use a photocopier.

Roughs

When you have briefed the graphic designer ask for, say, four roughs of the proposed design. These are sketches of possible designs incorporating the ideas you have discussed. They will not be finished artwork but will be complete enough to give you a good idea of what this will be like, with a clear indication of colour and how it will be used. Areas to be occupied by copy – typeset information – will only be roughly marked. Look at each of the roughs and decide:

■ which most adequately fulfils your objectives?

■ which conveys the strong selling points?

■ which is the best design for *your* production?

■ do not be afraid to start again if none of the roughs is suitable.

This process is not always easy. Do not make it more difficult by trying to do it by committee. Involve the director by all means as the person most in touch with the development of the production, but no one else is necessary.

When looking at the roughs think constantly of your list of strong selling points, particularly with reference to the relative prominence given to various elements in the design:

■ is the title as prominent and *clear* as it should be?

■ if the play is less well-known than the author is *his* name as prominent and clear as it should be?

■ is the design going to be equally effective on a poster – seen from a distance – and on a handheld leaflet?

■ is there too much on the design? (over-design is a far greater danger than under-design).

Leaflet roughs

COPYWRITING

The graphic designer will prepare *artwork* — a finished design ready for printing — from the rough you have chosen. This will go to the printer with the *copy* you have been assembling over the weeks. The copy is all the information about the production (when it is on, where, and how to book tickets) that will go on posters and leaflets. Make sure that the copy is ready well before the finished artwork, so that the printer is not kept waiting, and the print therefore delayed.

You will provide all the copy for *typesetting* — the process that puts it into the exact layout in which it will appear on the print. Some graphic designers have their own typesetting equipment, some ask the printer to do it. Either way, make sure that you get a *proof* — one example of what the copy will look like — so that you can check for mistakes. If you have second thoughts about some of your copy or if you have to add something important, you can amend the proof. *Try to do this sparingly because there will almost certainly be a charge for a change at this stage, if it is not the fault of the typesetter.* Because of this, you should assemble the copy over a long period of time so that you have a chance to check and up-date it. Do not leave it all until the day before it is due at the typesetter's as you may well leave out something important.

You will probably print posters, perhaps of different sizes, and a leaflet. They will share the same basic graphic image as it is both undesirable and expensive to have a different design for each. So a single-sided leaflet can be identical to the poster; it is a very straightforward process for a printer to reduce artwork to various sizes. If you use both sides you can be more expansive on the reverse, but you should check out the relative costs of printing on one or both sides, and decide accordingly.

For the poster (and therefore also for the leaflet), and separately for the back of the leaflet, if it is printed on both sides, you should provide the answers to these six questions:

☑ WHO ARE YOU?

☑ WHAT ARE YOU SELLING?

☑ WHERE IS IT HAPPENING?

☑ WHEN IS IT HAPPENING?

☑ WHY SHOULD ANYONE BUY A TICKET?

☑ HOW CAN ANYONE BUY A TICKET AND HOW MUCH WILL IT COST?

The greatest danger in assembling copy and in checking proofs of copy is not that you will provide false information; if you check carefully enough mistakes can be identified. It is that you will leave out something of vital importance. This will not happen if you make sure you have answered the six questions above, both when you submit the copy and when you check the proofs.

Answer each question briefly but adequately, on the poster and the front of the leaflet, and more fully on the back of the leaflet. Do not worry about duplicating information on the two sides.

Who?

Your group's name in its own typeface, with its logo if there is one. If you are new, explain who you are and what your policy is.

What?

The title and the author. If the play is in copyright, check whether you are contractually obliged to print the author's name in a certain size of type and whether there is a compulsory way of describing the play.

Where?

The name of the venue and its full address, including telephone number, however well-known you think it is. Use the venue's logo if it has one. On the back of a leaflet print a map if the venue is not well-known.

When?

The dates, *including the year*, the days and the times. Do not just give inclusive dates: not everybody will know that you do not perform on Sundays, for example. If you have space, a performance diary is the clearest way of describing your schedule and is, of course, more important the more complicated your performance times. Be consistent in your use of the twelve- or twenty-four-hour clock.

Why?

The impact your poster has will depend to a large extent on the simplicity and clarity of the image. You should not add too much copy about the play, just a compelling one-line description. You can expand on the reasons why someone should buy a ticket on the back of a leaflet. This is a crucially important part of your campaign because anybody who reads it has already demonstrated a degree of interest in the play by picking up the leaflet. Tell that person what the production is about, in such a manner as to convert them from a potential to an actual ticket-buyer.

Although you must emphasize what is positive, you should not intentionally mislead. The benefit of this will only be short-term. The ticket-buyer will feel cheated and will be much less likely to trust you or your successor next time. You should have in mind a long-term relationship with your audience based on trust and reliability. Your copy need not be long: 100-150 words is usually ample. When writing it refer constantly to your list of strong selling points, and be specific. A sentence such as 'Shakespeare's witty and enchanting comedy' describes at least five plays and is therefore meaningless without more explanation or reference to your production.

How?

The answer to the 'how' question is usually the most technically difficult to provide simply and clearly. Ticket prices and concessions are usually complex and seem even more so when put together. A general rule is not to print all the details of prices, concessions and box office arrangements on posters. An indication of the price range with the box office telephone number(s) will suffice. The back of the leaflet, however, must have complete and accurate information. Do not fall into the trap of being unclear in an attempt to reduce the amount of copy. Write out the seat prices and concessions available for each performance so that you have all the necessary information on one sheet of paper. Simplify it carefully by bracketing sets of prices and concessions that go together. Do not delete any information that is not conveyed clearly somewhere else.

Gradually refine the way you are presenting the information until it is as simple and clear as it can be. If you are performing in an established venue, it will have its own box office arrangements which you should describe as simply as possible, going through the same process as for ticket prices and concessions. You are probably presenting a lot of detailed information which can look extremely intimidating, even to someone who is an experienced theatre-goer, so make it as easy as possible to read. Divide it into sections, each with its own heading:

☑ PRICES

☑ CONCESSIONS

☑ BOX OFFICE ADDRESS AND PHONE NUMBER

☑ HOW TO BOOK BY PHONE – POST – IN PERSON

☑ CREDIT CARDS

☑ SPECIAL OFFERS

USING THE PRESS

Most members of the public will learn about your project through the press, whether in paid-for advertisements, press stories or reviews. You should co-ordinate those three elements so that you make maximum use of the opportunities they present. To a large extent you have control over when and how each of those three appear and, although to a lesser extent, how they look.

Whenever possible use your logo image and standard title typeface in advertisements, press releases or any other communications with the press. Bear in mind that the use of an image in an advertisement might make it larger, and therefore more expensive. It will also, of course, make it more effective but you should use this device sparingly.

ADVERTISING

If you are performing in an established venue you might be committed to its regular advertising for which you will pay indirectly one way or another.If you are arranging your own it can be extremely expensive, even in small local newspapers. The cheapest advertising rates are not necessarily the best value if the circulation is small. Ask about circulation when you are checking out the rates and compare the different newspapers and magazines available to you on a value-for-money basis. You will have to make quite difficult decisions about whether to place a lot of small advertisements or fewer larger ones. As a general rule larger (display) advertisements are more effective in the earlier part of a campaign. By the time the play is on you should be able to reduce to non-display (lineage) size ads.

If sales are going very badly just before opening night one way to boost them would be to revert to larger display ads. You are paying for this service and have complete control over when they appear. You can, if you want to, make the opening of booking coincide with a large ad, for example. You can also discuss with the newspaper where your ads will appear on the page. If the newspaper misprints *anything* you should ask for another free entry as compensation. Use your logos and images whenever possible and experiment with 'reversing out'

some or all of the ad. This is a process where what is normally printed black on white is printed white on black and it can be extremely effective. Do all your ads answer the six questions on the previous page?

If you get extremely good notices, but are not doing such good business that you can stop advertising you can add a few words or lines from the notices to your ads.

Monitor advertising during the run. If you sell out you can cancel advertising and save money – unless you want the prestige of advertising that you are sold out (good for your long-term image). If there is a particular performance that is proving difficult to sell you can concentrate advertising on that. As with the rest of your campaign, be flexible.

PRESS STORIES

Press stories are free advertisements and you should aim not only to get as many as possible but to maximise your control of them. You should decide *what* the stories are, *when* they appear, *what* they say, and *how* they look. They should never be events that the press discover and tell you about. In a sense you will be creating the stories. Some will have a double purpose: a story saying that you are looking for a particularly bizarre or rare prop might actually produce that prop. Even if it does not you will have had a story in the newspaper. Think of stories that relate your production, however obscurely or indirectly, to the locality. Always when giving out a story make sure the reporters you speak to have in writing the correct details of the name of the play, venue and performance details, and remind them tactfully to include them in the story.

PHOTOGRAPHS

You are more likely to get a story in the newspaper if you suggest the possibility of a photo opportunity. Fortunately theatre projects offer a great variety of these. In particular look out for the possibility of using colour photographs if any of your local newspapers have a colour section. If you are doing a period play with particularly colourful costumes, for example, this will look attractive if photographed against the background of a local building of the period in which the play is set. Do not assume that the reporters you deal with will be knowledgeable about plays or the theatre. In a local newspaper they will deal with a wide variety of subjects, and the arts are often a long way down on their or their editor's list of priorities. So you will have to explain things clearly and carefully, and sometimes take part in stories or photo sessions which are more vulgar than you would ideally like them to be.

Photo sessions

Ask the newspapers if they can send a photographer to a photo call for the show. This is not a stunt but a specially arranged session where a number of photographers will take photographs of the show in, as it were, performance. You must decide what minimum number of photographers will make this exercise worthwhile, but even only one or two will be valuable. Even if they do not use a photograph you will be fostering a relationship with the press that will be useful in the future. Also, you may be able to make use of them yourself in other ways – newspapers normally sell copies of all photographs taken for a scale fee.

Arrange the photo session with the production team well in advance, and especially make sure that the production manager/stage manager build it into the schedule. By doing that you will be more likely to get full costumes, wigs, make-up and the correct set to photograph against. A very good time for this is immediately before a dress rehearsal. Out of courtesy to the director, discuss what two or three pictures would be good, even if you know already.

Bear in mind that neither the photographer nor you will have much time (probably no more than thirty minutes) so you must avoid having to change costumes or scenery during the photo session. Some photographers will ask you to pose people whereas some prefer you to run a short scene, perhaps repeating a particular part of the action several times. Ensure that the photographer has made an accurate note of the names of the actors, the characters, the title of the play, your group and the performance dates. The newspapers may use these photographs for a news item saying that the play is opening, or with a review. Whatever, it is

a free large display advertisement and will be well worth any disruption it may have caused the production schedule.

REVIEWS

You cannot tell reviewers what to write, but you can create conditions in which they will be favourably disposed to the production.

First identify your 'press night' – the performance where you will invite reviewers. It will normally be the first performance, but might not be if you are having a preview. Generally speaking the second performance of a comedy will be better reviewed than the first because the actors' timing will be slicker. Discuss this with the director, who will probably have strong feelings about it, but do not be persuaded to have a press night later than you know to be right. You have to take into account when the reviews will appear: you want them as soon as possible especially if it is a short run and you must be in time to catch weekly newspapers, whose deadlines are sometimes earlier than daily papers'.

If you know who the reviewers are, invite them by name. If not, invite their editors by name and they will pass on the invitation. Use the play's typeface and image on the invitation.

Do not send tickets. Ask the reviewers to phone to say they are coming and how many tickets they want so that you can make contact. Ask them to collect the tickets from you at a certain place in the foyer before curtain-up so you can meet them.

When they arrive ask them to join you for a drink in the interval(s), which most will be happy to do. Give them a choice of red or white wine or soft drinks.

Do not talk about the production unless they do. Ask them if they can use a photograph with their review and if they can, give them one that is labelled on the reverse with the name of your group, the name of your play and the names of all the actors and their characters. If they have sent a photographer to the photo call they will already have one.

BOX OFFICE

The box office is your sales outlet and is a crucially important part of your marketing campaign. Until the actual performance it is the only point at which there is contact, however indirect, between your group and the public. You may be performing in an established venue where the box office staff are not normally treated as part of the marketing operation. In this case it is even more important that you do so, even if it means doing it tactfully and discreetly. Before you finalize your seat-pricing structure and leaflet copy about it, make a point of discussing it with the box office staff, the people who will have to implement it. Explain your aims. Tell them what the show is like and encourage them to ask you questions about it, the kind of questions the public will ask. You will learn something about how to put your copy together, and the box office will be more likely to be able to answer the public's questions accurately and helpfully.

During the booking period make a point of visiting the box office regularly, partly to assess how well sales are going (although the sales figures will tell you that), but also to make yourself accessible for queries. There may be problems that you had not anticipated before going to print, and the sooner you know about them the better.

Working without a box office

If you are performing in a venue without its own box office, and therefore have to start from scratch minimize the problems you are likely to have. If there are local ticket agencies, use them. They will charge a commission on sales, (perhaps as much as 10 per cent), but they will be worth that expenditure. Treat the agencies as if they are your box office in terms of the briefing described above. You will probably have to provide an allocation of tickets for each agency.

Unless you have a very small seating capacity and a short run, do not use home-made tickets. If you have numbered seats and a variety of prices and concessions, professionally printed tickets are very important. Go to a printer who has the capacity to print tickets. Alternatively, an inexpensive way of printing tickets is to use a computerised box office system that has the capability to print tickets with the names of different groups and productions.

Once you have printed your tickets you can, of course, set up your own box office in addition to any agencies you might use. It may be particularly useful to operate your own priority booking system for members of your group or any others to whom you want to extend that special privilege. If you intend to operate such a box office on a longer-term basis – a whole booking period could be four weeks or more – be sure that you have the capacity to staff it.

Direct selling

Investigate the possibilities of direct selling – that is taking the box office to the public rather than expecting the public to come to you. It is surprisingly easy to organize and is effective both as a way of selling tickets and as a way of publicizing your project. Find out where there are large gatherings of people who are potential ticket buyers. In a college, the common rooms or dining halls at meal times are good places, the latter especially if you can place yourself near a queue. If the beginning of an academic year is coming up this is an opportunity not to be missed. Organize it on these lines:

■ identify your direct selling site

■ get permission to sell in it

■ set up a temporary box office. A simple table with a display board covered in posters behind it can look effective

■ you can also use your box office as an information centre, but the prime aim is to sell tickets. You will sell more if you have a special offer which is only available at that time and in that place.

Because direct selling can only be done for very short periods and is simple to organize, it is something that volunteers can easily do.

PROGRAMMES

A programme of whatever size or sophistication fulfils three functions:

■ it is a formal communication to the audience, telling them things they need to know, some of which may be statutory

■ it is a guide to a theatrical event and enhances the audience's enjoyment of that event

■ it is a souvenir of the event.

In planning your programme, which you should do from the start of your marketing campaign, bear all three functions in mind.

If you are in a venue which prints its own programmes you will be told how much space you have in it for editorial – that is non-advertising material – and what the deadline is for submission of copy. The venue may give you the option of printing your own programme. If it does not, and you would particularly like to, ask for it.

If you are printing your own programme, build it into your marketing campaign in terms of both the schedule and the budget.

BUDGET

You will probably not want to subsidize your programme, so cost it at least to break even. As in other budgeting calculate your income first. You will have an idea of likely audience numbers. Calculate that one in three of the general public will buy a programme. A much smaller proportion of school parties will buy one, probably one in ten.

You then have to play around with figures, while you assess what kind of programme to print. You have the choice of anything from a free, or very cheap, single sheet giving minimal information to a highly sophisticated full-colour souvenir programme book.

A way of increasing programme income is to include advertising. Assess how much you can generate and build that amount of space into the programme. Take care that the extra you are paying to print the advertisement will be more than covered by the advertising income.

When you have given some thought to the amount of material that will go into your programme an idea of its likely size and cost will emerge. You can then calculate the income by determining its price and with a few adjustments, if necessary, you will have a basic budget for your programme.

DESIGN

As with the other printed material in your campaign, programmes can be significantly enhanced by advice from a graphic designer or from a printer. Among the things that can make a simple programme look more sophisticated are:

■ imaginative layout and typesetting

■ using coloured paper instead of white

■ using photographs, or if you cannot afford them, line drawings (of say, costume designs)

■ printing on both sides of a single sheet of paper and folding it rather than having a stapled booklet. This gives you larger expanses of paper for imaginative layout. Size A3 folded twice to form A5 is particularly effective.

Carry the logos and design images you have used on the poster through on to the programmes. The same artwork can be used for the programmes at very little extra cost.

DEADLINES

When discussing the programme with a designer or a printer settle very clearly what the deadlines are and make sure everyone who is providing material for it knows these dates. You *must* have a programme for the first performance and it must be complete and accurate. Programme slips can be used if you omit something important or in an emergency but they should be avoided.

CONTENTS

The content of the programme falls into four categories:

Compulsory

There will be some things that you have to include in your programme. You will find out about them principally from your theatre licence and, if the play is in copyright, the licence to present it from the author's agent. This category includes:

- statements relating to emergency exits and gangways
- the correct description of the play
- credit for the author.

There may also be credits which you are contractually obliged to print including those for:

- funding from any source
- sponsors
- suppliers who have lent or given anything to the production. Make sure that the stage manager tells you who these suppliers are before your deadline.

Production

Those who have created the production have to be adequately credited. This can be a minefield because it can involve a great many people who will be hurt if they are not included. Start a register of production credits at the earliest opportunity, and update it constantly. Consult closely with the production/stage manager about technical credits.

The cast list presents both problems and opportunities. Consult the director. Bear in mind that as well as providing a record of the distribution of roles, it can help to clarify a play. It is very common to print characters 'in order of appearance'. But for a large-cast play (Shakespeare especially), it is more helpful to set out the characters in a way that enhances understanding of the action. In

Henry V, for example, you could set out separately the king and his followers, the French and the commoners. In *Romeo and Juliet* you could, by listing them separately, explain who the Capulets and who the Montagues are, and thus make much of the play a good deal less confusing.

Extra editorial

This is material intended to explain the background to the production of the play:

- extracts from books used as source material
- photographs of rehearsals or of source material for the design
- costume or set drawings
- a piece written by the director.

Always give plenty of notice if you ask someone to write an original piece for the programme, especially the director who will be very busy.

Make sure to clearly label or head everything so that the reader has no doubt what it is and how it relates to the production.

Get permission to use any non-original material from books or other sources if it is in copyright. (Copyright runs for 50 years after the death of the author.)

Advertising

When you solicit advertising for the programme tell advertisers *when* you need the copy and ask for *camera-ready artwork*. This will mean that you can give it straight to the printer for immediate processing without any other work being necessary.

CHAPTER II

VENUE AND FRONT OF HOUSE

Choosing a venue for your production is as important as choosing the play itself. Your group may have its own venue with its own well rehearsed systems.

If you have been doing shows in the same venue for many years now might be the time for a change, either in the way you use that venue or in the venue itself. Like everything else in administration – budgeting, financial control, marketing – you must be specific in the way you choose and present your venue and organize its house management. If you have your own venue you can not only improve the ways in which it serves

the public but also adapt it so that it more closely matches the particular play you are presenting.

If you do not have a venue you can start from scratch to find the site that comes closest to your ideal venue. You will have to make a judgement about the advantages and disadvantages it is bound to have. Broadly, if it offers all the facilities you would like, it will probably be too expensive. If it is inexpensive, it will in some ways be inadequate. Set out here are the most important criteria to consider when finding a venue. You will also have your own based on the specific requirements of your production.

CONVENTIONAL VENUES

Theatres, art centres and concert halls – buildings designed for public purposes and managed either professionally or non-professionally – are usually available for use by various groups. These venues have obvious attractions in that they have:

■ trained experienced staff (from whom you can learn) to help you
■ sophisticated lighting, sound and stage equipment
■ a marketing operation that you can slot into and its own audience, of whatever size
■ a high public profile.

On the other hand the resident staff will do some of the work you might like to do for yourself. The organization, depending on its size, may not be as receptive to your ideas or as flexible as you would like it to be. Also you will, of course, be paying for all the services it offers, directly or indirectly

Many groups will take the view that, in the normal course of events, a theatre is an ideal venue, and that the advantages outweigh the disadvantages. The major factor you will need to assess is financial, that is whether or not you can afford to hire the venue. This will depend in its turn on the nature of the agreement you enter into with the theatre. There are three basic kinds:

1 The venue pays you a negotiable fee for presenting the play with an understanding that you get a percentage of the box office receipt over a certain level. With this kind of deal you would agree to pay a series of charges levied by the theatre to cover its staff, publicity and other costs. Such charges are usually called a *contra*, and do not necessarily have a fixed upper limit.

2 You split the box office receipts in an agreed percentage. You should receive the higher percentage – it can be anything between 55 per cent and 75 per cent – and the venue the balance. Contra charges may also be a part of this agreement.

3 You hire the venue for a negotiated sum which covers the facilities you have requested. You would keep the box office receipt. A contra would also be part of this agreement.

You must be extremely careful about contra charges. Ask specifically if there will be any, and ask for an estimate of what they will be. Include the likely contra charges in your expenditure budget. Do not subtract them from the income since that will distort your figures and give you misleading information for the future.

To get a reasonably accurate estimate of contra charges, and to give the theatre the information to calculate a hire fee in the last option, you must have as clear an idea as possible of your requirements in terms of access to the building – while you are fitting up (putting in) the production for example – and your use of its staff. This involves close liaison with your production/stage manager. Given that you are unlikely to get option 1, option 2 is fair to both parties, in that you share the risk and also the responsibilities for maximizing income, since it is in both your interests to do so.

UNCONVENTIONAL VENUES

Conventional theatre venues may not be available to you for a number of reasons: too large or too expensive; not available when you want them; or non-existent in your area. You may have to look elsewhere and in effect create your own theatre. You may choose to do this instead of using an available one. Either way, once you have decided to look at other performance spaces, you need to think about both the problems and the opportunities.

You can perform in virtually any space that can contain a stage and an audience area: halls, dining halls, the open air. You will almost certainly be hiring the venue so think carefully before deciding.

THE PROBLEMS
Licence
You will need to licence the space as a theatre, albeit on a temporary basis. You will

need a licence if you charge admission in any way – that is by selling tickets, selling programmes for admission or asking for a compulsory 'donation'. Find out where your local licencing authority is and discuss your ideas with their representatives. You might find that there are large costs (to do, for example, with emergency lighting) that you had not anticipated. Alternatively they might suggest solutions to problems that you thought were insoluble.

Staging and audience

The director and designer will concern themselves with the staging and the various kinds that are possible in unconventional spaces. You will be more concerned with the audience area although the two things are closely related particularly in respect of sightlines which in unconventional spaces can be a serious problem.

You may find that the pressure to increase stage size diminishes your seating capacity, and you must ensure that you have the ability to make the income that is necessary. If there is any disagreement on this issue, think positively about it and encourage the director and designer to do so also. There are many different ways of arranging the stage/audience relationship, and in an unconventional venue there will be more scope to be imaginative and flexible. In-the-round creates a surprisingly large seating capacity in an apparently small space, and some plays might lend themselves to promenade performances.

Lighting

This is principally the concern of the lighting designer and production/stage manager, but you might be involved in contractual negotiations relating to lighting. Is there sufficient power supply for stage lighting? If not you will have to organize it, pay for its connection and supply? Can you install stage lighting? Are there particular problems in fixing it to walls or pillars – this is often a difficult problem in churches.

Backstage

Is there sufficient room for dressing room and costume space, storage, stage management space?

Heating

Will you need heating, and is it adequate?

Front of house

Apart from audience seating, is there any space for a box office for door sales, a 'foyer' and for catering in the interval? Are there adequate cloakroom facilities?

Position

Is there adequate access, including that for the disabled? Is there car-parking nearby?

Examine all these potential problems *before* you start negotiating terms for the use of the venue because the cost of solving them could affect your ability to mount the project, and will certainly affect how much you are prepared to pay for the hire.

Be realistic about the problems, but also be, and encourage your director and designer to be, positive and creative. There are some venues that will adapt easily to theatre use, but some that won't. If, for example, you are in an old and attractive building, you might lose many of the benefits of using it if you try to obliterate its original features. In other words look for opportunities in the building which you can use to advantage.

THE OPPORTUNITIES

Matching production to venue

An unconventional venue can give an extra dimension to the play by providing the perfect setting – for example, As You Like It in the open air, or Midsummer Night's Dream as a promenade, open-air production.

Creative freedom

The space may lend itself to imaginative use and creative lighting, plus the opportunity for impressive design effects with very little set.

Public interest

An unusual project in an unusual venue will stimulate press coverage, and consequently public interest and ticket sales.

Sponsorship

The project is more likely to attract sponsorship because of its unusual nature the heightened public awareness.

HOUSE MANAGEMENT

There must be one person in the theatre, whenever the audience is present, who is legally responsible for ensuring that the terms of the licence are observed. That person is legally the licence holder or someone else nominated in writing to be responsible. That nominated person will normally be the house manager.

As the licence holder or nominee this person will be responsible for:

■ the safety of the public
■ their comfort
■ creating the right conditions for their enjoyment of the production

Safety

The starting point in matters of safety will be the licence. It will stipulate conditions to do with the provison of exits, the width of gangways and their obstruction, and emergency lighting. Whoever actually provides these features – the lighting person or production/stage manager – the house manager is *legally* responsible for ensuring that they accord with the terms of the licence. Especially in an unconventional venue the licencing authorities will have made a special visit before granting a licence and will have made their conditions very clear. So if you are the house manager but not the licence holder make sure that you know *exactly* what these conditions are. Although you will hope never to have to do so, the abilitiy to evacuate the theatre quickly in case of a fire or other emergency is a vital element in the safety of the audience.

Comfort

Your audience will expect and should get an entertaining and *comfortable* evening. They are more likely to enjoy the play if they are in a warm, well-ventilated, clean venue with comfortable seats.

If you are in an unconventional venue – a church or the open – this may seem difficult. In fact it offers many opportunities to enhance the audience's enjoyment. If the heating is inadequate or non-existent ask them in the leaflet to bring blankets, which you might

also offer for hire for a small fee. Do the same with cushions. If they know about these things in advance they will join in the spirit of the occasion and enjoy it all the more.

Be particularly aware of the various needs of people with disabilities by providing for example, ramps for wheelchairs and special positions *with a good view of the stage.* Check before each performance with the box office to see if disabled people have booked and, if they need help, look out for them.

Catering can be as simple or as complex as you care to make it. You can offer coffee, tea, soft drinks and confectionery in the intermission or you can be more ambitious. Selling alcohol is not as difficult as you might think. Of course, check out the licencing requirements, preferably while you are enquiring about the theatre licence. You can simplify it, if you prefer, by offering a limited variety of drinks, say in a wine bar. Simplest of all you could ask a local bar to provide a service for you in which case they would get their own licence and keep the profits, but you would be providing a service for your audience.

If you want to limit the amount of work during the intermission you could include a glass of wine or something non-alcoholic in the price of the ticket. You would then know how many glasses of wine to prepare and no further money need change hands. You will have to think of this well in advance to include it in the publicity and when assessing the ticket price.

Unless you have a lot of space and the right equipment, avoid hot food. You can provide a good range of attractive and nutritious cold foods using volunteers. You could also arrange for special meals before or after the performance at a nearby restaurant, which should be happy to co-operate in getting extra business. Make a feature of this in your publicity.

Staff and procedures

The key to the provision of a safe and comfortable experience for the audience is your front of house staff. In terms of the licence they are there in the interests of safety, principally to help evacuate the audience in case of any emergency. In practice they will rarely do that, but will fulfil many other functions concerned with the audience's comfort.

Your licence may well tell you how many attendants to have. The number may be related to the seating capacity or the number of exits or both. As a general rule do not have fewer than two for every 100 members of the public as they will have to:

■ examine tickets, tear them and keep the stubs
■ describe how to get to the seat or actually show the person the way
■ sell a programme and handle the money

This is a surprisingly difficult sequence of events for one person, and it can help to divide the duties. Do this in relation to the layout of your venue and the likely flow of people. For example if you have a 100-seat auditorium with two main entrances, put two attendants at each one to deal with tickets and point people in the right direction. Have two more walking up and down the gangways to get them seated and sell programmes.

One or two attendants should always remain in the auditorium during the performance, again in case of any emergencies.

Training is crucial even if you are only doing a few performances. Gather your attendants before the first performance (invite them to a dress rehearsal so that they get to know the show) and take them through their duties. Make sure that they know where the seats are: people entering a theatre are under mild stress, and nothing makes them feel more insecure than an attendant who is as much in the dark as they are. Get them to work out individually how they are going to hold the ticket stubs or programmes. Make or buy wallets to fix around their waists for holding cash. Make sure that they know exactly what they are doing so they project confidence.

Carry out emergency evacuation drills at least once a week, or with each new set of attendants. The licencee or nominee is solely responsible for a decision to evacuate in case of fire or other emergency. No-one else can take or should influence that decision once taken. The licencee will:

■ inform attendants that the theatre is being evacuated; they will go to their pre-show positions
■ walk on stage and say words to the effect 'Ladies and gentlemen for reasons entirely beyond our control we cannot continue with tonight's performance. Although there is no immediate danger please leave the theatre as quickly and calmly as possible via the exit closest to you'. The attendants will then open the doors and guide the audience out of the theatre.

Depending on the urgency of the situation the licencee may also say 'Please contact the box office tomorrow about arrangements for refunds or alternative tickets.'

Some tips for the staff

Ask them all to greet patrons with a smiling hello or good evening. They will soon get used to doing it and the effect on the public is extremely positive. Also, if you don't have a uniform, ask them to wear similar clothes – say black trousers or skirts and white shirts. Make badges of your group's logo.

In case of a complaint you will have to exercise your own judgment about the situation and take action, if any. Very often a patron will not expect you to do anything except listen (to interrupt would only add fuel to the fire). Let it run its course and then respond. Only argue a point if you are convinced of the facts. Customers are not always right but they think they are.

Starting the show

As house manager you decide when to start the show and restart it again after an intermission. Communicate this decision to the stage manager or other person on the book:

Your aim is to start it at the advertised time or as soon as possible thereafter. Three factors might delay this decision:

■ A queue at the box office. Patrons in such a queue will probably co-operate if you ask them to, by speeding up their transaction. They will be more willing if you tell them that the show will not start without them

■ A queue at the doors
■ A problem inside the auditorium, perhaps someone occupying the wrong seat.

You *cannot* start a show if any of these factors applies. If you do, the opening scene will be disrupted and the rest of the audience and the actors will be justifiably angry.

If you *plan* your doors, box office and attendants carefully you are less likely to encounter such difficulties. As you approach the starting time be aware of the three possible problem areas and look out for them. You will not be attached to any particular place: your job is to 'float' and sort out these problems.

Refer constantly to the box office's seating plan. Should you reach the starting time without a crisis but with a substantial section of the audience missing you have to make the very difficult decision of whether to hold the curtain. On the whole there should not be a great many individuals missing. If there are two rows missing, a glance at the plan will probably confirm that it is a party. You won't know whether or not they will definitely be turning up if you wait for five or ten minutes. If they don't you have wasted time and you will still have to cope with latecomers. Should you decide to delay for a few minutes tell the stage manager so that he or she can warn the actors.

The problem of latecomers

Make sure that in the leaflet and on the tickets you point out that latecomers may not be admitted until a suitable break in the performance if it would cause a disturbance.

Discuss with the director a suitable point for the admission of latecomers, which might be at the end of the first or second scenes. If your attendants come to a dress rehearsal they will know that point in the show.

Just before the start of the show check where the empty seats are so that you and the attendants know where to put latecomers to avoid leading them all around a dark theatre.

When the latecomers arrive commiserate with them; do not be disapproving. They will be angry with themselves anyway. Explain that the show has started and ask if they mind waiting.

Tear their tickets and tell them where they are going to sit, *outside the auditorium*. Ask them to be extremely quiet and take them in at a suitable point.

When the time for the admission of latecomers arrives the attendants inside should open the doors as quietly as possible to take them in. The attendants outside should stay where they are.

Extras

Your aim throughout the marketing campaign and the organization of your venue has been to reflect the specific qualities of your production. Plan extra events in and around your venue which would include:

■ giving the audience a complete evening out, that is more than a performance of a play, however good
■ enhancing the audience's enjoyment and understanding of the play

There are several areas you can explore.

Catering

Even if you do not intend to commit yourself to very sophisticated catering you can often make it more interesting by relating it to the production. This works well for a comedy or musical, but not for a serious play. If you have a bar you could create a special cocktail for the production. Or there might be a traditional dish that is appropriate to the play (perhaps one from its country of origin) and comparatively easy to prepare and serve. Use your imagination and have fun with your ideas. One warning: do not expect large numbers of people to drink your special cocktails or eat your special food. Most will not, but they will be amused and impressed at the trouble you have gone to.

Music

Having appropriate music playing in the foyer as people come in and during the intermission is another good way of enhancing audience enjoyment. Live music is preferable and there are bound to be local

musicians who will be happy to perform fee of charge or for a nominal fee. Again, this is something more appropriate to lighter productions. It will improve the atmosphere in a foyer more significantly than any other single factor. Recorded music is a second-best option and, if it is a commercial recording, will be subject to a licence fee.

Photographic exhibitions

As a matter of course you should have production photographs to exhibit in the foyer and other parts of the theatre. Although photographing a show is not easy, there will be someone who is happy to do it for you. Avoid posed shots: that's how they will look. The photographer should ideally attend a dress rehearsal to watch the play and get an idea of the action and what would make good photographs. The photographer should then attend a second dress rehearsal and take plenty of photogaphs – perhaps up to a hundred – feeling free to move around to get the best angles. He or she should then produce contact sheets, very small prints of the photographs, so you can choose which to have printed full size.

Ask the photographer to try to do this by the first performance . Avoid colour photographs unless your photographer is very proficient. Productions with very colourful sets and costumes tend to look garish and vulgar whereas productions with very dark colours look better. Try to choose photos which feature all the performers without revealing a particular piece of action which is best kept as a surprise for the audience.

Other exhibitions

Other material can also be exhibited to give background information about the play or the production. It can relate to and supplement the material, if any, that you have in the programme. An exhibition is a particularly good way of providing information about a very serious play as it gives patrons the opportunity to think about it before or during the action.

Merchandising

Merchandising – the selling of articles relating to the show or your group – is fraught with difficulty, and you should look at it extremely carefully. There is no limit to the ways in which you can promote yourselves: on T-shirts, mugs, ties, ashtrays, anything that people might buy as a souvenir or as a way of contributing to your funds.

But cost the merchandise very cautiously. Quotes from firms who print T-shirts, for example, will make it seem like a very profitable activity, but it is usually only so if you can make and sell many more than you probably will. Anything relating to the show will have a relatively short life, and will then be virtually unsaleable. Merchandise relating to your group will have a longer life.

If, having thought through all the problems you still want to proceed with your merchandise you should:

■ get as many sole outlets as possible, not just the foyer during the performance
■ treat the merchandise as part of the marketing campaign and budget it very carefully

Glossary

A

Anti-pros (US) see Front-of-House lights

Apron extension of stage beyond the proscenium

ASM assistant stage manager

Auditorium area in which the audience is accommodated during the performance

B

Backcloth cloth usually painted, suspended from Flies at the rear of the stage

Backing (1) cloth or solid pieces placed behind doorways and other openings on sets to conceal stage machinery and building (2) financial support for a production

Bar horizontally flown rod (usually metal) from which scenery, lighting and other equipment are suspended

Bar bells bells sounded in all front-of-house areas to warn audience that the performance is about to continue. Operated from prompt corner, and so usually written into prompt copy

Barndoor adjustable shutters attached to stage lights to control the area of light covered by a particular lamp

Batten (1) see Bar (2) piece of wood attached to flown cloth to straighten it and keep it taut (3) piece of wood joining two flats (4) a group of stage lights suspended over the stage

Beam light a light with no lens, giving a parallel beam

Beginners call given by deputy stage manager to bring those actors who appear first in the play to the stage

Bifocal spot spotlight with additional shutters to allow hard and soft edges

Black light ultra violet light

Blocking the process of arranging moves to be made by the actor

Board lighting control panel

Book (1) alternative term for the scripts (2) the prompt copy (3) the part of a musical show conducted in dialogue

Book flat two flats hinged together on the vertical

Booking closing a book flat

Boom a vertical lighting bar

Boom arch used to hang a lantern from a boom

Border flown scenic piece designed to conceal the upper part of the stage and its machinery or equipment

Box set setting which encloses the acting area on three sides. Conventionally in imitation of a room in which the fourth wall has been removed

Brace portable support for flats

Bridge walkway above the stage used to reach stage equipment

C

Call (1) warning given at intervals to technicians and actors that they are needed on stage (2) notice of the time at which actors will be required to rehearse a particular scene

Callboard notice board on which calls and all other information relevant to the production should be posted

Cans headsets used for communication and co-ordination of technical departments during a performance

Centreline imaginary line drawn from rear to front of stage and dividing it exactly in half. Marked as CL on stage plans

Channel a circuit in the lighting or sound system

Chase a repeated sequence of changing lighting states

Check to diminish the intensity of light or sound on stage

Cinemoid a colour medium or filter

Circuit the means by which a lantern is connected to a dimmer or patch panel

Clamp C or G clamps are attached to lights to fasten them to bars

Cleat fixing on the back of flats to allow them to be laced together (cleated) with a sash line or cleat line. Also a metal fly rail to which ropes are tied

Clothscene scene played before downstage drop or tabs, while a major scene change takes place

Colour call the list of coloured gels required for a lighting design taken from the plan of the lighting design

Colour frame holder for the colour medium or filter in front of the light

Colour Medium translucent filter material placed in front of lights to give a coloured illumination

Colour wheel in lighting, a device attached to lamps which, when rotated, charges the colour medium through which the light is shown

Come down (1) instruction to actor to move towards the audience (2) instruction to lower intensity of sound or light (3) end of performance; time when curtain comes down

Corner plate triangle of plywood used to reinforce the corners of a flat

Counterweights mechanical system used for raising and lowering flown scenery

Counterweight flying the system of flying scenery, lights etc., whereby the flown item is balanced by counterweights

Crossfade the practice of moving to a new lighting or sound effect without intervening darkness or silence: one effect fades out simultaneously with the new one's being brought into play

Crossover (1) the device on a sound system that routes the sound of the correct pitch to the correct part of the loudspeaker; (2) the space behind the stage setting or below the stage through which actors can get from one side of the stage to the other without being seen by the audience

Cue (1) verbal or physical signal for an actor to enter or speak a line (2) point at which an effect is executed or business takes place

Cue light box with two lights, red and green, which warn an actor or technician to standby (red) and then do (green) whatever is required of them. Ensures greater precision when visibility or audibility is limited

Cue sheet list of particular effects executed by one department in a production

Cue-to-cue rehearsal of technical effects in a production with actors. The scene is rehearsed in sections beginning with a cue for standby, and concluding when the effect is finished

Curtain call process of actors appearing at the end of the play to receive audience applause. Formerly actors were called before the curtain by the audience

Curtain speech out of character address to the audience by a cast member or participant

Curtain up (1) time at which a play begins (2) a call given to the company to warn them the performance has begun

Cut cloth vertical scenic piece cut to reveal more scenery behind it. Most common in musicals

Cutting list list of materials required for scenery and set construction together with the correct dimensions of the pieces

Cyclorama undecorated backing to a stage, usually semi-circular and creating a sense of space and height. Often some theatres have permanent or standing cycloramas which have actually been built. The term is always abbreviated to cyc

D

Dead (1) the point at which a piece of scenery reaches the desired position onstage (2) a redundant production or scenic element

Decibel dB the measurement of volume of sound

Diffusion (colour) used like a gel but to soften and spread the beam of light rather than to colour it. Also called a frost

Dim the process of decreasing the intensity of light onstage

Dimmers the apparatus whereby lights are electrically dimmed

Dip small covered hole in stage floor with electric sockets

Dock area at side or rear of stage where scenery is stored when not in use

Downstage part of stage nearest to audience

Dress circle also known as the circle. Area of seating above the stalls and below the balcony

Dressing items used to decorate a setting

Dress parade the final check of costumes before the first dress rehearsal. The cast parade each of their costumes in order before the Director and Costume Designer so that any final alterations can be made

Drop suspended cloth flown into stage area

DSM deputy stage manager

Dutchman (US) thin piece of material used to cover the cracks between two flats

E

Elevation a working drawing usually drawn accurately and to scale, showing the side view of the set or lighting arrangement

Ellipsoidal the type of reflector used in many profile spots

Entrance (1) place on a set

through which the actor may appear (2) point in the script at which an actor appears

Exit (1) the process of leaving the stage (2) point in the script at which an actor leaves the stage

F

Fader a means of controlling the output level of a lantern (lamp) or amplifier

False proscenium construction placed behind the real theatre proscenium for decorative or practical purposes

Fit-up installation of lighting, technical equipment and scenery onstage when coming into a theatre

Flash-out system to check whether the lights are functioning properly by putting them on one at a time

Flat scenic unit comprised of wood or stretched cloth applied to a timber frame and supported so that it stands vertical to the stage door. Door flats and window flats have these openings in them. Masking flats are placed at the outer edges of the acting area to disguise areas of the stage from the public

Flies area above the stage in which scenery, lighting and other equipment are kept. If whole backdrops are to be stored then the flies should be at least twice the height of the stage opening

Floodlights also called floods. Lights which give a general fixed spread of light

Floorcloth painted canvas sheets placed on the stage floor to give a specific effect

Floor pocket (US) see dip

Flown (1) scenery or equipment which has been suspended above the stage (2) flown pieces are any scenic elements which will be made to appear or disappear from view in sight of the audience

Fly the process of bringing scenery in and out of the stage area vertically

Flying (1) the process of stocking the flies (2) special effects whereby actors are suspended by wires to create the illusion of flying

Fly floor gallery at either side of the stage from which the flies are operated

Floats see footlights

Focusing the process of fixing the exact area to be lit by each light onstage

FOH Front-of-house. Any part of the theatre in front of the proscenium arch

Follow spot light directed at actor which can follow all movements

Footlights lights set into the stage at floor level which throw strong general light into performers' faces downstage

Fourth wall imaginary wall between audience and actors which completes the naturalistic room

French brace support for scenery fixed to stage

Fresnel type of spotlight with a fresnel lens which gives an even field of light with soft edges

Frontcloth see cloth

Front-of-House lights lights hung in front of the proscenium arch

Frost see diffusion

G

Gauze painted cloth screen, opaque when lit from the front, that becomes transparent when lit from behind. Often used at front of stage to diffuse total stage picture

Gel Colour medium introduced before light to alter colour of beam

Get-in/out (US) see fit-up process of bringing scenery into or taking it out of the theatre

Ghost a beam of light which inadvertently leaks from a light and falls where it is not wanted

Gobo (1) screen introduced before a stage light to give a particular image onstage (2) cut out shape that is projected

Green room general area in which cast and crew wait during performance

Grid metal frame from which all flying equipment is suspended

Groundrow raised section of scenery usually depicting bushes rocks etc.

Grouping (US) see blocking

H

Half half hour call. Warning to company given thirty-five minutes before performance

Handprop any prop handled by an actor, such as a handbag, walking stick, umbrella

Hanging attaching flying pieces to appropriate bars

Hook clamp the device that holds a lantern onto a bar

Hot lining the method by which lanterns, bulbs and cables are checked during rigging

House (1) audience (2) in opera, the entire theatre, and by implication, the company

I

Impedance a term for the electrical resistance found in a/c circuits, thus affecting the ability of a cable to transmit sound as electrical pulses. Measured in ohms

In one (US) see clothscene

Inset a small scene set inside a larger one

Iris a device within a lantern which allows a circular beam to be altered through a range of sizes

Iron a fire proof curtain that can be dropped downstage of the tabs in case of fire. Today it is usually made of solid metal and is electrically operated

K

Kill instruction to cease use of particular effect in lighting or sound

L

Ladder a ladder-shapped frame used for hanging side lights. It cannot usually be climbed

Lamp unit of lighting equipment

Lantern see lamp

Left stage left. That part of the stage to the actor's left when he is facing toward the audience

Leg cloth suspended vertically from flies and used to mask sides of stage and small areas within it

Levels (1) indicates intensity or volume of light or sound (2) raised areas onstage used for acting

Limes jargon for follow spots and their operators

Line drawings (US) see technical drawing

Linnebach projector used for projecting a picture from a gel or glass slide onto the set. Often used to give a shadow effect

Load in/out (US) see get in/out

Lose to turn off lighting or sound, or to remove an article from the set

Luminaire international term for lighting equipment. Not restricted to theatrical lighting

M

Marking (1) in use of props or scenery, the deployment of substitutes for the real object during rehearsal (2) in singing, a

means of using the voice with reduced volume and without vocalising extremes of register (3) any account of a role in which the full powers are not being used by the performer in order to save resources

Maroon a pyrotechnic giving the effect of a loud explosion

Mark out the system of lines and objects set on a rehearsal room floor to indicate the exact position of scenery and furniture. Marking out is the process of doing this

Mask to hide or conceal unwanted areas or machinery. Also used to describe one actor obscuring another unintentionally

MD musical director

Memory memory board. An advanced type of lighting control system where the required levels are stored electronically

Mezzanine area of seating above the orchestra and below the balcony. When a theatre has only a single balcony, first several rows are frequently designated the mezzanine

Mixer sound controls desk, used to mix and adjust levels of sounds from various sources

O

Offstage any backstage area not seen by the audience. Most specifically used to indicate the areas at the actor's right and left

OP opposite prompt. Stage Right (US Stage left)

Orchestra (US) see stalls

Out flying term for up

Overture (1) the music which begins a performance (2) a call to the actors and technicians that the performance is about to begin in a musical work

P

PA system the public address or any sound amplification system

Pack a number of flats all stored together

Pan (1) movement of lighting from side to side (2) used to describe water-based stage make-up (pancakes) (3) term (now nearly obsolete) to describe theatre sound installation

Parcan type of lantern which holds a par lamp

Patch border panel a panel at which the circuits governed by individual lighting dimmers can be changed

Perch lighting position concealed behind the proscenium

Periactus a tall, prism-shaped piece of painted scenery which can be revolved to show various phases

Pipe (US) see bar

Places please (US) see beginners

Platform (US) see rostrum

Plot (1) commonly used to describe the action of a play (2) any list of cues for effects used in the play

PM production manager

Practical any object which must do onstage the same job that it would do in life, or any working apparatus e.g. a light switch or water tap (faucet)

Preset (1) used to describe any article placed in its working area before the performance commences (2) also describes a basic lighting state that the audience sees before the action begins

Projector (US) see floodlight

Prompt copy fully annotated copy of the play with all the production details from which the show is run each time it is performed

Properties props. Any item or article used by the actors in performance other than costume and scenery

Props skip basket or cupboard in which props are kept when not in use

Props table table in convenient offstage area on which all properties are left prior to performance and to which they should be returned when dead

Pros proscenium arch the arch which stands between stage and auditorium. A pros arch theatre is a conventional theatre with a proscenium arch, usually without a forestage

PS prompt side. Conventionally meaning stage left, the term now refers only to the side of the stage in which the prompt corner will be found. In the US the PS is generally stage right

Prompt corner desk and console at the side of the stage from which the stage manager runs the show

Pyrotechnics any chemical effects used onstage or in wings to create lighting or special effects

Q

Quarter back stage pre-show call given twenty minutes before curtain up (ie. fifteen minutes before beginners)

R

Rail bottom or top batten of the frame of a flat

Rake the incline of a stage floor away from the horizontal; a raked stage is higher at the upstage end than at the downstage

Readthrough early rehearsal at which the play is read without action. Usually accompanied by discussion

Reflectors the shiny surfaces in the back of lighting equipment which help intensify the beam

Rigging the means of fixing lamps to appropriate bars before lighting a production

Right stage right. That part of the stage to the actor's right when he is facing the audience

Risers the vertical part of a stage step

Rostrum a raised platform sometimes with a collapsible frame used for giving local prominence to certain areas onstage

Run (1) the number of scheduled performances of a work (2) abbreviated form of run through

Runners a pair of curtains parting at the centre and moving horizontally

S

Saturation rig an arrangement of lights in which the maximum number of spotlights is placed in every possible position

Scatter the light outside the main beam of a spot

Scrim (US) see gauze

Seque musical term indicating that one number should go immediately into the next

Set to prepare the stage for action. To set up is to get ready. To set back is to return to the beginning of a given sequence

Shutter device in front of lamp to alter shape of beam

Single purchase counterweight flying system where the cradle travels the same distance as the fly bar's travel. The counterweight frame therefore occupies the full height of the side wall of the stage

Sightlines the angles of visibility from the auditorium

SM stage manager

Snap line chalk line, chalked piece of string which when stretched tight is used for making straight lines on stage

Special piece of lighting equipment whose main function is to perform a particular effect

Spiking see marking

Spill unwanted light onstage

Spot spotlight. Light giving a small circle of light, the dimensions of which can be precisely controlled by focusing

Stagger-run runthrough at which the production is pieced together, aiming at fluency but allowing for corrective stops

Stalls floor level area of seating in the auditorium

Strike instruction to remove any redundant or unnecessary object from stage

Super non-speaking actor not specifically named in the text

Swag curtains or tabs gathered together so they do not hang straight

Switchboard board from which lights are controlled

T

Tabs theatre curtains, most usually the House curtain

Tabtrack metal track on which the tabs run allowing them to open and close

Tallescope extendable ladder on wheels used in rigging and focusing lights and for minor corrections to flown pieces

Teaser short flown border used to mask scenery or equipment

Tech technical rehearsal at which all technical effects are rehearsed in the context of the whole production

Theatre in the Round acting area with audience on all sides

Throw in lighting, the distance between a light source and the object lit

Thrust stage type of stage which projects into the auditorium so that the audience can sit on at least three sides

Tilt the vertical movement of light

Tormentor (US) see teaser

Trap hole cut in stage and concealed by floor allowing access from below. Grave traps are usually double traps creating the illusion of a grave or pit. Once a common part of all theatres traps are now becoming increasingly rare

Trapeze single short hung lighting bar

Treads the flat part of stage steps

Truck movable cradle upon which scenery is placed to facilitate its movement

U

Upstage in a proscenium or thrust stage the area furthest away from the audience

W

Wagon (US) see truck

Walk-through rehearsals at which actors go through entrances, moves and exits to make clear any changes or alterations made necessary through change of cast or venue

Warning bells (US) see Bar bells

Ways the maximum number of combinations of channels on a lighting installation

Wings the sides of the stage concealed from the audience's view

Work-out in a dance or movement rehearsal, a vigorous session to prepare the body for specific work

Workshop any non-performing backstage area of a theatre

Workshop performance a performance in which maximum effort goes towards acting and interpretation rather than sets or costumes

Musical theatre special glossary

Andante walking space

Allegro happily, lightly

Allargando getting broader

Coda last section of music, often in a different tempo or mood

Cadence the resolving chords in music

Largo broadly

Lento slowly

Maestoso majestically

Presto fast

Aria solo, usually reflective in content

Duet musical number for two singers

Trio three singers

Quartet four singers

Ensemble (1) together (2) place in which all the characters all sing together

Finale (1) the end (2) by extension, a musical sequence which ends each act, often comprising different musical material but having an overall shape

MD musical director

Band parts the individual copies required by each player in an orchestra and containing only the notes for their particular instrument.

BIBLIOGRAPHY

Listed below are a representative selection of books for each of the titles in this series.

In the United Kingdom Spotlight publish annually *Contacts*, a complete guide to the British Stage, TV, Screen and Radio (7 Leicester Place, London WC2. Tel: 071 437 7631)

In the United States the Theatre Communications Group Inc. (TCG) (355 Lexington Avenue, New York, NY 10017. Tel: 212 697 5230) has a publications department which publishes not only plays and books but also a monthly magazine of news and features called *American Theatre*. It also publishes an employment bulletin for the performing arts called Art SEARCH.

Bentley, Eric *Theory of the Modern Stage*, London, 1968

Brook, Peter *The Empty Space*, London, 1985

Brown, John R *Drama and the Theatre*, London, 1971

Hoggett, Chris *Stage and the Theatre*, London, 1971

Oren Parker, Smith, W L, Harvey R *Scene Design and Stage Lighting*, London, 1979

Stanlislawski, K *An Actor Prepares*, London, 1981

Costume and Make-up

Barton, Lucy *Historic Costume for the Stage*, Boston, 1938

Barton, Lucy *Period Patterns*, Boston, 1942

Corson, Richard *Fashions in Hair*, London, 1985

Corson, Richard *Stage Make-up*, New York 1960

Cunnington, Phillis and Lucas, Catherine *Occupational Costume in England*, London, 1967

Directing a Play

Berry, Cicely *Voice and the Actor*, London and New York, 1974

Hagen, Uta and Frankel, Haskel *Respect for Acting*, New York, 1980

Hodgson, John and Richards, Ernest *Improvisation*, London, 1978; New York, 1979

Nicoll, A *The Development of the Theatre*, London and New York, 1966

Willett, John *The Theatre of Bertolt Brecht*, London, 1983; New York, 1968

Lighting and Sound

Bentham, Fredrick *Art of Stage Lighting*, London, 1980; New York, 1968

Burris-Meyer, H and Mallory, V *Sound in the Theatre*, New York, 1979

Moore, J E *Design for Good Acoustics*, London, 1961; New York, 1979

Pilbrow, Richard *Stage Lighting*, London and New York, 1979

Reid, Francis *Stage Lighting Handbook*, London, 1982; New York, 1976

Stage Design and Properties

Govier, Jacquie *Create Your Own Stage Props*, London and New York, 1984

Leacroft, Richard and Helen *Theatre & Playhouse*, London, 1984

Molinari, Cesare *Theatre Through the Ages*, London and New York, 1975

Oren Parker, W L Smith, Harvey, R *Scene Design and Stage Lighting* London and New York, 1979

Stage Management and Theatre Administration

Baker, Hendrik *Stage Management and Theatre Craft, (3rd Edition)*, London and New York, 1981

Bond, David *Stage Management: A Gentle Art*, London 1991

Crampton, Esme *A Handbook of the Theatre*, London and New York, 1980

Gruver, Bert *The Stage Manager's Handbook*, New York, 1972

Reid, Francis *The Staging Handbook*, New York, 1978

SUPPLIERS AND STOCKISTS

Listed below are a representative selection of suppliers and stockists.

UNITED KINGDOM

Costume, Props and Make-Up

Angels and Bermans
40 Camden Street
London NW1 0DX
Tel: 0171 387 0999
Fax: 0171 383 5603

Bapty and Co. Ltd (weapon hire)
703 Harrow Road
London NW10 5NY
Tel: 0181 969 6671
Fax: 0181 960 1106

Borovick Fabrics Ltd (theatrical)
16 Berwick Street
London W1V 3RG
Tel: 0171 437 2180/0520
Fax: 0171 494 4646

Bristol Old Vic Hire
Units 1 and 2
Hayward Road Industrial Estate
Staple Hill
Bristol BS16 4NT
Tel: 0117 970 1026

Brodie and Middleton (dyes, canvas, metal powders and other paints)
68 Drury Lane
London WC2B 5SP
Tel: 0171 836 3289
Fax: 0171 497 8425

Freed of London Ltd (theatrical shoes)
94 St Martin's Lane
London WC2N 4AS
Tel: 0171 240 0432
Fax: 0171 240 3061

Laurence Corner (period hats and other unusual clothing)
62 Hampstead Road
London NW1 2NU
Tel: 0171 813 1010
Fax: 0171 813 1413

Lighting and Sound

DHA Lighting Ltd
3 Jonathan Street
London SE11 5NH
Tel: 0171 582 3600
Fax: 0171 582 4779

Jim Laws Lighting
West End Lodge
Wrentham
Beccles
Suffolk NR34 7NH
Tel: 0502 675 264
Fax: 0502 675 565

MAC (Sound Hire)
1 and 2 Attenburys Park Road
Altrincham
Cheshire WA14 5QE
Tel: 0161 969 8311
Fax: 0161 962 9423

Northern Stage Services Ltd
Unit 1, Trent Industrial Estate
Duchess Street
Shaw
Oldham OL2 7UT
Tel: 0170 684 9469
Fax: 0170 684 0138

Strand Lighting
Grant Way
Isleworth
Middlesex TW7 5QD
Tel: 0181 560 3171
Fax: 0181 568 2103

Theatre Project Sound Services
13 Field Way
Bristol Road
Greenford
Middlesex UB6 8UN
Tel: 0181 813 1112
Fax: 0181 566 6365

White Light Electrics Ltd
57 Filmer Road
London SW6 7JF
Tel: 0171 731 3291
Fax: 0171 371 0806

Stage Equipment

British Harlequin
Kent House
High Street
Farningham DA4 0DT
Tel: 0132 286 5288
Fax: 0132 286 4803

CCT lighting
Hindle House
Traffic Street
Nottingham NG2 1NE
Tel: 0115 986 2722
Fax: 0115 986 2546

Flint Hire and Supply Ltd
35 Queen's Row
London SE17 2PX
Tel: 0171 703 9786
Fax: 0171 708 4189

Northern Light
39 Assembly Street
Leith
Edinburgh EH6 7RG
Tel: 0131 553 2383
Fax: 0131 553 3296

Northern Light
79 Loanbank Quadrant
Govan
Glasgow G51 3HZ
Tel: 0141 440 1771
Fax: 0141 445 4406

Rex Howard (Drapes) Ltd
Acton Park Industrial Estate
Eastman Road
The Vale
London W3 7QS
Tel: 0181 740 5881
Fax: 0181 740 5994

UNITED STATES

It is impossible to give a comprehensive list of suppliers and stockists in the space available. Those wishing to find a specific supplier should consult *Theatre Crafts Directory* (P.O. Box 470, Mt Morris, Illinois 61054 - 0470). This publication gives a comprehensive list of suppliers for costume fabric, electrical supplies, dance-wear, curtains and drapes, film equipment, and flameproofing. It even lists about 50 suppliers of feathers for theatrical costumes!

Costume, Props and Make-Up

Norcosto Inc.
3203 North Highway 100
Minneapolis
Minnesota 55422
Tel: 612 533 2791
Fax: 612 533 3718

Stagecraft Industries
5051 North Lagoon Avenue
Portland
Oregon 97217
Tel: 503 286 1600
Fax: 503 286 3345

Tobins Lake Studios
7030 Old US 23
Brighton
Michigan 48116
Tel: 810 229 6666
Fax: 810 229 0221

Wolf and Co.
4301 Bryan Street 309
Dallas
Texas 75204
Tel: 214 823 1880
Fax: 214 823 5659

Lighting and Sound

Electronics Diversified
1675 NW 216th Avenue
Hillsboro
Oregon 97124
Tel: 503 645 5533
Fax: 503 629 9877

Hub Electric Inc.
6207 Commercial Road
Crystal Lake
Illinois 60014
Tel: 708 530 6860
Fax: 815 455 1499

Showco Inc.
201 Regal Row
Dallas
Texas 75247
Tel: 214 819 3100/630 1188
Fax: 214 630 5867

Stage Equipment

Peter Albrecht Corporation
6250 Industrial Court
Greendale
Wisconsin 53129 - 2432
Tel: 414 421 6630
Fax: 414 421 9091

INDEX